BOY, HAVE I GOT PROBLEMS!

KAY ARTHUR
JANNA ARNDT

HARVEST Kids™

HARVEST HOUSE PUBLISHERS
EUGENE, OREGON

Illustrations by Steve Bjorkman

Cover by Left Coast Design, Portland, Oregon

SFI Certified Sourcing
www.sfiprogram.org
SFI-00453

Discover 4 Yourself® Inductive Bible Studies for Kids

BOY, HAVE I GOT PROBLEMS!

Copyright © 2000 by Precept Ministries International
Published by Harvest House Publishers
Eugene, Oregon 97402
www.harvesthousepublishers.com

ISBN 978-0-7369-0148-2 (pbk.)
ISBN 978-0-7369-3130-4 (eBook)

Printed in the United States of America.

17 18 19 20 /ML-BG/ 26 25 24 23

To Chase and Brent Arndt, my precious sons.
Thank you for being patient and giving so unselfishly,
for all your help trying out our ideas, and
especially for those words of encouragement!
This one is for you. Third John 1:4.
I love you,
Mommy

CONTENTS

BOY, HAVE i GOT pROBLEMS!

Help! Ellie, our advice columnist, just got the flu. We have tons of mail and no one to answer it. Can you help us? I know filling Ellie's shoes is a big job (she wears a size 11), but I'm sure you can do it because the answers to all these kids' problems can be found in God's Word and with the help of His Holy Spirit. In addition, you have this book. It's called an inductive Bible study. That word *inductive* means that this Bible study is set up for you to discover *for yourself* what the book of James means. Instead of someone else telling you what the book is about, you'll look at the Bible passages and figure it out for yourself. And that's just what our readers need—someone to answer their questions straight from God's Word. So if you're ready, let's open the first letter.

THiNGS YOU'LL NEED
▼

NEW AMERICAN STANDARD BIBLE (UPDATED EDITION)
PEN OR PENCIL
COLORED PENCILS FOR OBSERVATION WORKSHEETS
INDEX CARDS
A DICTIONARY
THIS WORKBOOK

1

JAMES 1:1-11

Okay, we're ready for our first letter. This one is from a guy named Confused. Let's see what he has to say.

Dear Ellie,

I wanted to try out for the basketball team next week, but yesterday at practice I fell and broke my leg. Now there is no way I can make the team. I am so disappointed. I have been praying for this chance for a year. Why would God let this happen to me? I try to obey His Word.

Signed,

Confused

Wow! Confused seems to need your help. What an awful thing to break your leg during basketball practice after all that hard work! No wonder he is confused and wondering why God would let this happen to him.

We need to get an answer to him right away—God's answer, not ours. So let's turn to James and begin. James is a letter that God had written and included in His book, the Bible, to help people with their problems.

But before we begin, first things first. We need to pray. Bible study should always begin with prayer. We need God's help not only to understand His Word, but also to help other people answer their questions in a way that's pleasing to God. Take a moment to pray, and then we're ready to take our first look at James.

OH, THOSE TRIALS

Turn to James 1 on page 129. The pages with the Bible text on them are called Observation Worksheets. We will use them to do our Bible study.

Today, when we read a letter we don't usually know who

the writer is until we see the signature at the end. In Bible times, the writer of the letter identified himself immediately. Instead of waiting till the end, the letter was signed at the beginning!

Watch! Read James 1, verse 1, and see who wrote this letter and what he tells us about himself.

James 1:1 WHO wrote this book?

_____

HOW does he describe himself?

He is a _____ of God.

WHAT does it mean to be a bond-servant of God and the Lord Jesus Christ?

_____

FROM SLAVE TO BOND-SERVANT

In Old Testament times, a slave that had served his time under Jewish law would be set free. That slave could go to his master and say, "I know I have served my time and that you have to release me according to the law, but living in your house is better than living on my own. I would rather be your slave than be set free."

The master would take the slave and place the slave's earlobe against the doorpost and drive an awl through it. An awl was a thick metal spike with a sharp-pointed end. When the master pulled out the awl, there was a hole that everyone could see. It was too big for an earring! When everyone saw this hole they would know that this slave had an awesome master because this slave had chosen to stay with his master and serve him rather than being set free! This made the slave a bond-servant for the rest of his life.

To be a bond-servant means to be a love slave for life.

A bond-servant is a person who has chosen to be a slave after he has been given his freedom.

James is saying that he is God's bond-servant.

He has totally surrendered his life to serve God and Jesus.

Now, let's see. To WHOM is James writing?

James 1:1 _____

WHERE are the twelve tribes?

James 1:1 _____

The WHERE question you just answered gives us a chance to talk about something important called *context*. When you study the Bible, it's very important to understand the context of a passage. Context is a setting in which something is told or found. For example, where would you find a bed in your house? In the kitchen? No, of course not! You would find a bed in a bedroom. A bedroom is the context for a bed. When you look at context in the Bible, you look at the verses surrounding the passage you're studying. You also think about where the passage fits in the big picture of the whole Bible. Context includes:

- the place where something happens

- the time an event occurs (you sleep in a bed at night and cook meals in the kitchen during the day)

- the customs of the group of people involved

- the time in history an event occurred

Sometimes you can discover all these things from just the verses you're studying. Sometimes you have to study other passages of Scripture. It's always important to be on the lookout for context because it helps you discover what the Bible is saying.

AWAY FROM HOME

The twelve tribes are the Jews.
Being dispersed abroad means the Jews who believed in Jesus were living in foreign countries. The Jews were living someplace other than Israel—the land that God had given them for their permanent home!
These Jews had been scattered to other countries because of the difficult times for people who believed in Jesus.

James 1:2 WHAT does James call them?

_____

Brethren means "brothers." Now we know that all the Jews could not be James' blood brothers! They didn't all have the same parents. James is calling these Jews his brothers because they are his brothers in Christ. Their father is God because they have believed that Jesus is the Son of God.

James' Christian brothers had problems, and he wanted to help them. When we don't solve problems the right way, we can sin. And that makes God very sad!

Now that we have discovered who James is and to whom he's writing, let's read his letter and see what he has to say about problems (or trials as James calls them).

Read James 1:2-4.

Does verse 2 say *if* we encounter trials or *when* we encounter trials?

_____

Did you know the Bible was written in Greek? That's because Greek was the language that was used in much of the world at the time the New Testament was written. Looking at Greek words and their meanings can help us understand what the writer intends when he uses certain words. Let's look at the word *trials* in James 1:2. The Greek word for *trials* is *peirasmos*, which means to put to the test. A trial is a hard time that God allows to happen to us for our good. If one of your friends is mean to you, that would be a trial. God could use that trial to help you remember to be kind to others.

Why don't you try saying this Greek word? It's pronounced pi-ras-mos. Practice saying it to your friends. The next time you go through a trial, you can say *peirasmos!* Then you can share with your friends what the Bible says about trials. Isn't that a neat way to share God's Word?

In verse 2, James tells us to do WHAT when we encounter trials?

Consider it _____ _____.

WHAT are some of the trials—the hard or difficult situations—you and your friends run into?

1. _____

2. _____

3. ___ _____

And when they happen, what does God's Word say you are to do?

Consider it all ___ ___ ___! (Spell it out.)

Isn't that amazing? Not only should we expect problems, James tells us, but we should be joyful about them. He also says we will have many trials.

Read James 1:3-4. WHY do Christians have trials?

Knowing that the _____ of your _____

produces _____. And let _____

have its _____ result, so that you may be

_____ and _____, lacking in nothing.

God allows us to have problems to test our faith—to help us become more like Jesus, perfect and complete.

Right off the bat we see that James tells Confused what he needs to know about problems. Now that you've studied God's Word, let's answer Confused's letter.

Dear Confused,

Ellie is out sick with the flu. My name is_____, and I'm helping answer Ellie's letters while she is sick. I am so sorry to hear that you broke your leg right before basketball tryouts. I know that God's Word holds all the answers to life's problems. I've been studying the book of James, a letter to Jewish Christians about problems.

Let me share with you what I learned today. In James 1:2, James tells us to consider it all_____ when we encounter various_____. That means that as Christians we can expect to have unplanned _____.

Even though trials are painful, like not being able to make the basketball team, they are for our good. God has a purpose for us during a trial. Verse 3 tells us that trials _____ our _____, and produce _____. Verse 4 says, "Let endurance have its _____ result, so that you may be _____ and _____, lacking in _____."

This verse shows us how much God loves and cares about us. He wants us to grow up to be mature and complete. God uses trials in our life to test our faith, to see if we are trusting in Him. I am going to memorize this verse so I'll be ready the next time problems pop up. Why don't you memorize it, too?

> *I understand your disappointment that you didn't get to try out for the basketball team. I would be disappointed, too! But remember, keep trusting in God.*
>
> *Signed, _____*
>
> P.S. *We'll write again once we have done some more studying in James.*

 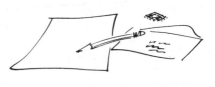

Here's the verse that you told Confused about. It's a great verse to memorize, isn't it? After all, everybody has trials!

James 1:2-4
Consider it all joy, my brethren, when you encounter various trials, knowing that the testing of your faith produces endurance. And let endurance have its perfect result, so that you may be perfect and complete, lacking in nothing.

Now write James 1:2-4 on an index card and carry it with you. Read it out loud three times a day—morning, lunchtime, and evening—and by the end of the week you'll have it memorized. Why don't you try saying it to a friend? Ask your friend to check you to see if you are saying the verse right. When you ask your friend to help you, your friend will get to hear this verse, too. You'll be sharing God's Word with your friend! Once you have God's Word hidden in your heart, you'll be ready to face anything. You won't be as likely to let things disappoint you or take away your hope.

LET'S UNLOCK THE DOOR. . .

We have a stack of mail on our desk. Boy, have people ever got problems! But before we open any more mail, we need to find some more answers to help Confused. Let's look at the letter James wrote to the Jewish believers to see what we can learn about God and why God would let this happen to Confused. Remember to pray before you begin!

Turn to James 1 on page 129. Today we are going to look at key words. Key words are words that pop up again and again. They are important in helping us understand the meaning of the Bible passage. Key words help us to unlock the door and discover what James is telling us in his letter.

- Key words are words that are repeated.

- Key words are important.

- Key words are used by the writer for a reason.

Every time you find a key word, you need to mark it by coloring it its own color or by using a symbol.

Here are some helpful ways to mark the following key words (or you can make up your own symbols). Just remember to keep them simple.

God (also, Lord) (purple triangle, colored yellow)

faith (blue book, colored green)

~~trials~~ (red fire)

<u>wisdom</u> (colored yellow, underlined orange)

Also remember to mark any other words that mean the same thing as the key word, such as pronouns.

PRONOUNS?

Pronouns are words that take the place of nouns:

Brent went to the park. *He* played soccer.

The word *he* is a pronoun because it takes the place of Brent's name in the sentence.

Watch for these other pronouns when you are marking key words:

I	you	he	she
me	yours	him	her
mine		his	hers

we	it
our	its
they	them

Hang in there—you can do it!

Great job! Tomorrow we will begin to see what we have
discovered by marking these key words.

P.S. Don't forget to practice your memory verse!

WHO IS GOD?

How should we begin?
That's right—we should pray first!

Now turn to page 129 and look at James 1:1-11. You'll see
that you marked the word *God* or *Lord* in these verses. After
you mark a key word, it's good to make a list of what you've
learned. Today we are going to make a list of the three things
you discover about God from James 1:1-11.
We've done the first one for you.

1. James 1:5 Ask God for wisdom.

2. James 1:5 _____

3. James 1:5 _____

Now let's go to other verses in the Bible and see what we
can learn about God. When we go to other verses in the Bible
to see what they say, this is called cross-referencing. Let's see
who God is. How can He save us?

Turn to Isaiah 14 in your Bible and read verses 24 through 27.

WHAT do we see about the Lord of hosts?

Isaiah 14:24 I have_____ so it has happened,

and just as I have _____ so it will stand.

Isaiah 14:27 The LORD of hosts has _____ _____,

and who can _____ it?

Now turn to Deuteronomy 32:39.

What do we see about God in this verse?

I am _____.

There is no god _____.

I _____.

I _____.

There is no one who _____.

Turn to Daniel 4:34-35. WHAT does King Nebuchadnezzar say about the Most High?

Daniel 4:34: The Most High is to be _____.

He lives _____.

His dominion is an _____.

His kingdom _____ from generation to generation.

Daniel 4:35: He does _____.

No one can _____.

No one can say, _____.

All theses verses show us that our God is sovereign, which means God rules over everything. There is nothing in this universe that God does not have total, absolute, and complete control over.

Everything that happens to us must first be okayed by God.

God created everything, and He is in control of everything.

Just think, *no one* can do anything to you without God's permission. Isn't that awesome!

Romans 8:28 says, "We know that God causes all things to work together for good to those who love God, to those who are called according to His purpose." This verse shows us that if we are God's children and love Him, all things (even bad things) will turn out for good.

What a great promise from God to encourage us when bad things happen!

Why don't you draw a picture of God ruling over everyone and everything to send to Confused? That way he will have a picture of who our Most High God is.

Way to go! Aren't you excited about all that you've seen today concerning our heavenly Father?

STANDING FIRM OR TOSSED BY THE WIND?

Have you practiced your memory verse today?

Then you're ready to turn to James 1 on page 129.

Today we are going to see what James 1:1-8 has to say about faith, wisdom, and doubting. Remember, Confused is doubting God. Don't forget to pray! Then read James 1:1-8.

Now let's look at what *wisdom*, *faith*, *doubting*, and *double-minded* mean.

Wisdom means knowing the right thing to do. You show wisdom when you make the right choice.

Faith means believing God. You believe what God says in the Bible, and it shows by the way you act. You decide to do what God wants you to do.

Doubting means you aren't sure about something.

Double-minded means you keep changing your mind. You are not sure what you think, so you go back and forth trying to decide.

1. James 1:3 WHAT does God test?

   _____

2. James 1:5 HOW are we to get wisdom?

   _____

3. Look in your Bible at Daniel 2:20-23 and write down
   WHY we should ask God instead of people for wisdom.

   Daniel 2:20 _____ and _____
   belong to Him.

   Daniel 2:22 It is He who _____ the pro
   found and hidden things.

4. James 1:5 Is God stingy about giving us the wisdom
   we have asked for?

   _____

5. James 1: 6 HOW are we to ask for wisdom?
   (Remember what you learned in the word box.)

   _____

6. James 1:6 WHAT pictures does James give us of a
   doubter?

   _____

7. James 1:7 WHAT will the doubter receive from the
   Lord?

   _____

8. James 1:8 HOW is the doubter described?

   _____

Now let's write another letter to Confused and share what we have learned about God, faith, wisdom, and doubting.

Dear Confused,

I just wanted to share with you what I have learned from studying James about God, faith, wisdom, and doubting.

God is sovereign. That means that He is in control of everything that happens to us, like your breaking your leg. Deuteronomy 32:39 says, "It is I who put to death and give life. I have wounded and it is I who heal." When I have trials, I am to go to God and ask Him for ____ _____ without _____. If I turn to God and believe what He says, trials will not be able to toss me around like the surf is tossed by the wind. God will give me the wisdom I have asked for to help me endure the trial. Just remember who God is, ask Him for His help, and lean on His promise in Romans 8:28 that He will use this circumstance for good.

I will be praying for you that God will use your broken leg to help you handle trials His way.

Asking in faith,

_____

Just for fun, see if you can solve this rebus. A rebus is a word puzzle that mixes pictures and words. When you combine the pictures and letters by adding or subtracting letters, you will end up with a new word.

Hint: The answer to this rebus is one of the verses you're memorizing this week.

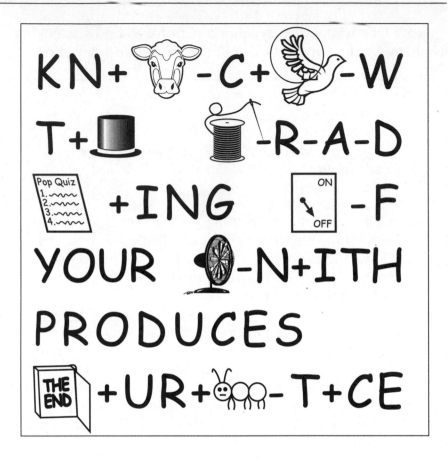

_____

_____

_____

You're doing great! We know that God is pleased with all your hard work.

P.S. Here's an exercise that you can do to demonstrate putting your trust in the right place—in God. Take a yardstick and try balancing it straight up and down while looking down at your hand. As long as you are looking at your hand (this represents trusting yourself), you cannot balance the yardstick. But if you look up at the top of the yardstick while trying to balance it, it works. This is just like looking up to God and putting your trust in Him, instead of in yourself.

RICH MAN, POOR MAN

The editor, Mr. Chase, just came by and said we have room for one more letter before the paper goes to print. So let's begin today by digging into our stack of mail and answering another letter for Ellie. But before we begin, let's remember to pray so that God can give us the wisdom that we need.

Dear Ellie,

Today at school I overheard some girls making fun of my clothes. It really hurt my feelings because I thought they were my friends. I would love to have clothes like theirs, but we don't have the money for expensive clothes. I feel so left out.

H. J.

Hurt and Jealous

Hurt and Jealous (HJ) needs our help. Let's turn to James 1 on page 129 and begin our study today by marking the key words listed on the next page.

rich man (green $)

humble (poor) (blue box and arrows pointing down, colored yellow)

Now that we've marked these words, let's see what God has to say about the rich man and the brother of humble circumstances (just like HJ).

Let's make a list.

Rich Man	Poor Man
_____	_____
_____	

Who do you think sees his need for God—the rich man or the poor man?

_____

This is a hard passage to understand, but it is important. From the list you made, you see that the poor man is to glory in his high position.

WHY would God think being poor is a high position?

_____

Let me ask you this: WHEN do you pray the most?

_____

Is it *when* you need help the most? _____

Isn't that when we run to God and put our trust in Him?

Now what about the rich man? WHAT is he to glory in?

_____

This means the rich man is to get excited when he sees his need for God. His need causes him to trust God.

What should we do for those who have needs when we have enough to share? Let's do a little cross-referencing by looking at Acts 2:42-46 at what the early church was doing.

Acts 2:45 WHAT were the believers doing?

_____

_____

Look up and read Acts 4:33-37.

Acts 4:34 WHAT does it say about the needy?

_____

Acts shows us that the early believers were selling their property and possessions and sharing them with anyone who had a need. As a result of this sharing, we see that there was not a needy person among them.

What about you? Is there something you can do to help someone who has a need, or who just doesn't have clothes as nice as yours?

Maybe you could be a friend to that person by inviting him or her over to your house.

Maybe you could give this person one of your special shirts or one of your skirts.

Why don't you pray and ask God for His wisdom in how you can help someone like Hurt and Jealous.

Now that we've studied God's Word about the rich and the poor, let's see if we can help Hurt and Jealous.

Dear Hurt and Jealous,

It hurt me, too, when I read your letter and saw how you've been treated. I am studying God's Word to help me know how to handle trials God's way. And you are definitely going through a trial, a test.

This is what I learned today about being rich or poor. God places His children in different circumstances. We are to boast in the position that God has put us in. If we are poor, we may not have money or the status that the world thinks is important, but we are rich in faith. We are a child of the King! The things we have on earth don't last, but being a child of the King is forever! If you were rich, you could have some big problems like trusting in your clothes to make you popular or accepted. If we are rich, we need to guard against trusting in what we have because those things do not last. We need to trust Jesus and follow Him only.

I know it hurts to be laughed at and to be left out. But God will use this hard time to make you more like Jesus. Just remember: You have a high position. You are a child of the King if you belong to Jesus!

I'll be praying for you and for the girls at school. I'm going to pray that they will learn it doesn't matter what you have, but to whom you belong.

Boasting in Him,

_____

Take some time now and ask yourself some questions.

How do you treat kids who are different than you?

_____

_____

Write a response below on how you should treat others who have less than you have.

_____

_____

_____

Well, it has been quite a week! Did you learn your memory verse? Did you say it to one of your friends? What did he or she think? Did it give you a chance to talk to your friend about Jesus?

Ellie and Mr. Chase are thrilled with all your hard work and help with the advice column. You're doing a great job!

2

SOMETIMES I'M TEMPTED TO DO WRONG

JAMES 1:12-27

We're off to a great start! We made our deadline last week. But more importantly, we helped our readers find answers to their problems by turning them to God's Word.

DAY ONE

STAND FIRM IN TRIALS

Let's begin today by looking at trials some more. Turn to page 129 and read James 1:12.

1. James 1:12 WHAT word is used to describe a man who perseveres under a trial?

_____

That means we are well off and happy if we persevere under a trial. Remember James 1:4? God is using trials to test us and make us perfect and complete. The Greek word for *persevere* is *hupomeno*, which means stay, to remain under the load or pressure. Can you say *hupomeno*? It's pronounced like this: hoop-om-en-o. Why don't you try saying it?

Have you ever seen a weight lifter in a contest? He walks up to the weight, lifts it, takes a breath, and then lifts the weight straight up over his head. He stands there with his arms stretched up high over his head, holding the weight as long as he can in order to win the contest. As long as the weight lifter is standing with the weight over his head, he is remaining under a very heavy load. He is persevering in order to reach his goal of winning the contest. The contest is a test of his strength. Our goal in persevering during a trial is to obey God and become more like Jesus. The test is to stay right where God has us and to trust Him.

2. Look again at the meaning of the word *persevere*. WHAT are we to do when we are under a trial?

    _____

3. According to James 1:12, a man who perseveres under trial is WHAT?

    _____

    He will receive WHAT? the _____ of _____

    which the Lord has promised to those who

    _____ _____

Being approved means that we will be found acceptable. So if we stand firm during the trial, we will be blessed and found acceptable by God. He will reward us with the crown of life. Isn't that awesome? Why don't you draw a picture to remind you of this important lesson? Or paste your picture in the box and draw a crown on your head! Show yourself trusting God and being accepted and rewarded by Him.

FiNAL EDiTION

Our memory verse for this week is James 1:22:

"But prove yourselves doers of the word, and not merely hearers who delude themselves."

Write this passage on an index card and practice saying it three times a day. Great job!

WATCH THOSE DESIRES!

Another letter has just come in that we should get to right away.

Dear Ellie,

Today at school a friend left her locker door open with five dollars lying on the top shelf. Even though I know it is wrong to steal, I was tempted to take the money. After all, who would know? Why would God let me be tempted like that?

Signed,

Feeling Guilty

Can you identify with "Feeling Guilty"? Have you ever been tempted to steal? We have.

Let's study James 1:12-18 to see if we can help Feeling Guilty by seeing what James has to say about trials, temptations, and God. Last week you marked your key words: *God* and *trials*. Today you need to turn to page 130 to James 1:13-14 and mark the key word *tempts* and *tempted* like this (red pitchfork). Now solve the crossword puzzle.

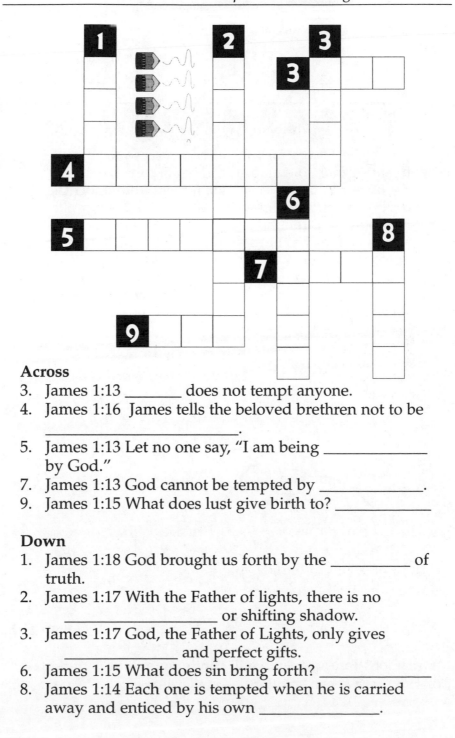

Across

3. James 1:13 _____ does not tempt anyone.
4. James 1:16 James tells the beloved brethren not to be

   _____.
5. James 1:13 Let no one say, "I am being _____ by God."
7. James 1:13 God cannot be tempted by _____.
9. James 1:15 What does lust give birth to? _____

Down

1. James 1:18 God brought us forth by the _____ of truth.
2. James 1:17 With the Father of lights, there is no _____ or shifting shadow.
3. James 1:17 God, the Father of Lights, only gives _____ and perfect gifts.
6. James 1:15 What does sin bring forth? _____
8. James 1:14 Each one is tempted when he is carried away and enticed by his own _____.

Tempted is a Greek word for luring fish out from under a rock.

The Greek word for *tempted* is *peirazo*, which means to entice, lure, to entrap. This is just like the picture of the fisherman trying to lure the fish out from under the rock. He tempts the fish with bait on a hook. Once the fish comes out from his safe place—the rock—and goes for the bait, he has been caught by the hook (temptations). We are the fish, and our safe place—the rock—is Jesus. We need to remain under Jesus and not be tempted by a baited hook (our desires), which leads to sin and death.

Great job! Tomorrow we will continue looking at temptations so that we can answer Feeling Guilty.

ACHAN IS TEMPTED

We can learn a lot from people in the Bible and how they handled temptations. Today, let's look at Achan in the Old Testament.

Achan was one of the children of Israel from the tribe of Judah. Let's turn to page 138 and read Joshua 6:17-19. Mark the key phrase *under the ban* by underlining it twice in black.

Joshua 6:17 WHAT is God's command to the children of Israel about the city (Jericho) when they conquer it?

_____

_____

Joshua 6:18 WHAT would happen if they took anything *under the ban?*

_____

_____

Joshua 6:19 WHO do all the silver and gold and articles of bronze and iron belong to?

_____

We see from Joshua 6 that there is a ban on everything inside the walls of Jericho. Everything was to be destroyed and nothing was to be taken. God had told the sons of Israel that all the spoils of war were forbidden at this time.

Now, let's read Joshua 7:1-26 on pages 138-141. Mark the following key words:

<u>under the ban</u> (underline it twice in black)

(Achan) (circle it)   sin (color it brown)

Joshua 7:1 WHAT did Achan do?

_____

Joshua 7:3-5 WHAT happened when the sons of Israel went up to Ai?

_____

_____

Joshua 7:6-9 WHAT did Joshua do?

_____

_____

Joshua 7:10-11 WHAT was God's response?

_____

WHAT did Israel do?

_____

Joshua 7:12 WHAT was the result of Israel's sin?

_____

WHAT were the three actions Achan said he did in Joshua 7:20-21?

1. I s __ __ __ __ __

2. I c __ __ __ __ __ __

3. I t __ __ __ t __ __ __

Joshua 7:24-25 WHAT happened to Achan?

_____

WHAT happened to his family and possessions?

_____

How did Achan handle temptation? He chose what he wanted over what he knew was right. When he was tempted, he allowed himself to be carried away by his own desires (lust).

Look at James 1:15 WHAT does lust give birth to?

_____

Did Achan sin? Look at Joshua 7:20. WHAT does Achan say?

"Truly, I have _____ against the LORD, the God of Israel."

Do you do what you want, like watching a TV show you have been told not to watch instead of what you know is right?

_____

Achan's sin didn't just affect him. It also impacted his whole family. It not only cost him his life, but it also cost his family their lives and the lives of 36 warriors. Achan's life teaches us some very important lessons:

1. Sin not only affects us but those around us.

2. God is to be obeyed, and He will judge sin.

3. Temptation comes from inside of us when we want our way instead of God's.

HOW can we handle temptations?

_____

_____

God gives us His promise in 1 Corinthians 10:13.

WHAT do we see about God in this verse?

God is _____.

God will not allow you to be _____ beyond

what you are able.

God will provide the _____ of _____ so

that you may be able to _____ it.

Now review what you saw about God in James 1:17-18.

God gives _____ gifts.

There is no _____with God.

God brought us forth by the _____ of _____.

Write a letter to Feeling Guilty about what we've learned concerning God's character, trials, and temptations.

Dear Feeling Guilty,

First of all, I'm proud of you that you didn't take the five dollars. Boy, you would have felt so guilty! God would have had to deal with your sin. Sin never goes unpunished! The temptation to take the money didn't come from God because the Bible says in James 1:13 that not only can God not be tempted by _____, but He Himself does not _____ anyone. We are tempted when we are carried away by our own _____. This is when we choose what we desire instead of what we know is right. The temptation comes from within. You were enticed by what you desired. We all are. Suddenly, we see something and want it! But is it right? No. Stealing is sin. God, who hates sin, never tempts us, but instead He's there to help us. We have to watch our feelings, thoughts, and desires, and do what God tells us to do in His Word. The next time you feel tempted, remember 1 Corinthians 10:13. God is faithful and will not allow you to be tempted beyond what you can handle. He will provide a way out. Go to Him and ask Him for help.

Leaning on Him in trials and temptations,

_____

Why don't you pray and thank God for giving only good and perfect gifts, for helping you handle trials His way, and for not tempting you?

P.S. Don't forget your memory verse!

WATCH THOSE FEELINGS!

The mail boy just brought in another bag of mail. Boy, people have lots of problems, don't they? Aren't you glad God has the answers? Let's go to the Lord and pray before we open another letter.

Dear Ellie,

Today, my mom sent me to my room because I got mad and yelled at her when she told me I was being disobedient. This isn't the first time it's happened. Can you tell me what I should do about losing my temper and saying things I really shouldn't say?

Signed,

Mad & Sad

Have you ever gotten mad and yelled at your mom? What did she do?

_____

What happened? Why did you get so mad?

_____

_____

What should you have done?

_____

How did you feel afterward?

_____

Let's go to James 1:1-20 on pages 129-130 and see what God's Word has to say about anger.

James 1:19 WHAT three things does he tell the brethren (God's people)? WHAT are they to do?
They are to be:

1. _____

2. _____

3. _____

James 1:20 WHAT do we learn about anger?

_____

Are you ready to answer Mad and Sad's letter?

Dear Mad and Sad,

I am sorry to hear that you lost your temper and yelled at your mom. In James 1:19 he tells us we are to be quick to _____ God's Word and to be slow to _____ and slow to _____. We know that letting anger rule us does not meet God's standard. Sometimes we get angry, which is okay as long as we do not sin. But yelling and showing disrespect to your mom is a sin. So what do you do now? Go to God and confess that you let your anger get the best of you and ask for forgiveness. Then go to your mom and ask for her forgiveness. Remember what James says about being quick to hear, slow to speak, and slow to anger. The next time you get angry, pray! Ask God to help you close your mouth and listen to your mom or whomever you are angry with. Don't answer back. Be quiet and count to ten. Take a deep breath and don't yell. If you talk when you are angry, it usually gets you in trouble. Tell God you want to please Him and be obedient to His Word. Ask Him to help you to be slow to speak and slow to get angry.

Growing in Him,

_____

Whew! That was a hard letter, wasn't it? We all fail at times to handle trials God's way. I am so glad that God is a good

God who loves us and is patient with us while we are growing up and getting to be more like Jesus. Why don't you go to God and ask Him to help you remember James 1:19-20 the next time you are put to the test?

BE A DOER!

Today we are going to start off by marking some more key words so that we can unlock what God wants us to know, to remember, and to do!

Let's mark every reference to the Word and its synonyms *word of truth* and *perfect law*. Sometimes different words can mean the same thing. For example, *sailboat*, a *yacht*, and a *rowboat* are all words for boats. Those words are called synonyms. In James 1 he uses several different words in talking about the Word, but they all mean the same thing. So read 1:18,21-25, and mark *word of truth, word,* and *perfect law* all the same way.

(blue book, colored green)

Now read the verses again aloud. When you say the words *hearers* and *doers* mark those words like this:

hearers (green ears)   doers (orange feet)

Now let's make a list of what we have discovered about the Word and what we're supposed to do in verses 21-25.

James 1:21 _____

James 1:22 _____

James 1:23 _____

James 1:25 _____

WHAT are we to do? (Watch the text.)

James 1:21 I am to p_ _ aside all

f_ _ th _ _ _ _ s and w_ _ _ _ _ _ _ _ s.

James 1:22 I am to be a d_ _ _ of the w_ _ d.

James 1:25 I am to l_ _ k i_ tent_ _ at the

p_ _ _ _ _ t l _ w, the l_ w of l _ _ er _ y

and a _ _ d _ by it.

James 1:26 I am to br_ _ _ e m_ t _ _ g _ _.

James 1:27 (Here's another list.) I am:

1. to v _ _ _ t o _ ph _ _ s and w _ _ _ _ s in

    their d_ _ t _ _ _ s.

2. to k _ _ p un _ _ _ _ _ ed b _ the w _ _ _ d.

We've learned a lot today about God's Word and about
what we are to do if we have a faith that is real.

Do you control your temper and your tongue?
___ yes ___ no ___ most of the time

Do you care about others?
___ yes ___ no ___ most of the time

Do you keep yourself unstained from the world by being careful about what you do? (For example, are you careful about what you watch on TV, the movies you see, and pictures you look at on the Internet?)
___ yes ___ no ___ most of the time

Are you a doer of the Word and not just a hearer?
___ yes ___ no ___ most of the time

What a tough but wonderful lesson! How about looking into God's mirror (the Word) and seeing if there is anything you want to ask God to help you with?

Write a short prayer to God asking for His help.

_____

_____

_____

_____

Thanks, friends, for all the help that you've given our readers this week! Hang in there—we still have lots more mail to go.

P.S. James says we should visit orphans and widows in their distress as a doer of the Word. Can you think of someone that you could help in your neighborhood or church? Could you visit someone in a nursing home or make a card reminding someone of Jesus' love? Ask your mom or dad to help you find a way to be a doer of the Word.

P.P.S. Here's an experiment to try. You will need paper, a marker, transparent tape, a toothpick, a clear glass jar that is flat on the bottom, water, pepper, liquid dish detergent.

Cut a piece of paper and write on it: "God's Word." Tape it to the bottom of the glass. Fill the glass jar with water. Make sure that you are able to read your message

through the jar. This is a picture of a believer who hears the Word and puts aside all filthiness, who keeps his tongue and anger in check. You can see "God's Word" clearly.

Now shake some pepper into the jar. The pepper is our filthiness and wickedness, such as the times we watch something we shouldn't watch, or yell at our brother or sister and pick a fight. Are you still able to see "God's Word" clearly?

Try to pick up some of the pepper with a toothpick. Try not to stir up the pepper. This shows what it's like when we do things our way.

Now put some of the liquid soap on the tip of the toothpick. Stick the tip of the toothpick into the middle of the water and see what happens. When we put aside all filthiness, we can clearly see God's Word.

3

SOMETIMES I'M NOT NICE

JAMES 2

Let's go to our desk and open the next letter. We have to help Ellie get another column ready for the paper.

Dear Ellie,

My friend is having a birthday party and inviting all the girls in our Sunday school class except one girl who my friend says is poor and would not fit in with the rest of us. I am afraid this girl's feelings will be hurt and she won't come back to church. What does God have to say about choosing favorites?

Caring and Concerned

pLAYiNG FAVORITES

What is the first thing we need to do? __ r __ y! We need God's wisdom and His answers to our problems.

What do you think about Caring and Concerned's letter?
Has anyone ever treated you differently because of who you are or what you have? Do you see friends do this at school or at church events?

Read James 2:1-9 on page 131 and see what he has to say about playing favorites.
Mark these key words:

poor (blue box with arrows pointing down, colored yellow)

rich (green $)

Now answer the following questions.

James 2:1 HOW are we *not* to hold our faith?

_____

James 2:2-3 WHO gets the special attention: the rich man or the poor man?

_____

James 2:4 WHAT had those people who made distinctions become?

_____

And WHAT were their motives?

_____

James 2:5 WHOM did God choose to be rich in faith and heirs of the kingdom?

_____

James 2:6 WHAT had they done to the poor man by treating the rich man better?

_____

James 2:8 WHAT is the royal law? (Hint: It's in the same verse in capital letters.)

_____

_____

James 2:9 WHAT are you doing if you show partiality (that is, choosing favorites) to rich people, to well-dressed people who have lots of things?

_____

Do you know kids who show partiality?

       yes   no (circle one)

How would you feel if they did it to you?

       happy   sad   mad (circle one or more)

How do you think God feels? Why? _____

_____

_____

We see that James is clear about how we are to treat one another. Write a letter to Caring and Concerned sharing what God has taught us today about playing favorites.

Dear Caring and Concerned,

I was really upset to hear about your friend's birthday party and so proud of you for being concerned. I am studying about playing favorites in James this week. In James 2, God commands us to not have personal favorites. He says if we treat people differently because they are rich or poor, we have made ourselves judges with _____ motives. We have dishonored the poor man and committed _____. As Christians, we are to fulfill the royal law which says, "You shall _____ your neighbor as _____."

I think you should go to your friend and share with her what you learned from God's perfect Word. Jesus wants her to treat other people the same way she would like to be treated. If your friend goes to church and studies her Bible and then treats the other girl this way, she is guilty of sin. It's just like she murdered someone! We must love other people no matter who they are or what they have. Is what this girl is about to do loving?

Look at James 2, verses 12 and 13. We see that we are following the law of liberty when we treat others the way we want to be treated. Those who show mercy will find mercy. Mercy triumphs over judgment. A Christian does not have to fear on judgment day because God's mercy forgives our sins. Our judgment will be overcome by God's mercy on us. We need to show other people this same mercy that God shows us. I will be praying for you and your friend.

In His love,

_____

P.S. Now that you have seen what God says about playing favorites, ask yourself if you ever play favorites.

Pray and ask God to help you fulfill the royal law.

Great work!

THE ROYAL LAW

Part of this week's memory verse is found in the puzzle on the next page. Starting with *Y* in the top left square, skip every other letter. Print the letters you land on in the blanks in the center of the puzzle.

Are you surprised that your memory verse is James 2:8 about fulfilling the royal law? Fill in the blanks of James 2:8 and practice saying it three times a day.

James 2:8

> *If, however, you are _____ the*
>
> *_____ _____, according to the Scripture,*
>
> *" _____ _____ love your neighbor as*
>
> *_____," you are _____*
>
> *_____.*

Why don't you draw a picture to go with our letter to Caring and Concerned? Show a way to fulfill the royal law.

We are so proud of all your hard work! And if we're proud, just think how God feels because you've been paying attention to His Word!

WHAT IS REAL FAITH?

Let's turn to James 2 on page 131 and read verses 1 through 26.

Today we are going to mark two key words in this chapter on our Observation Worksheet.

Faith (draw a blue book and color it green)

Works (color it blue and draw a pink box around it)

Great job! Tomorrow we will take a deeper look at what James has to say about faith and works.

WALK THE TALK

Today let's look at all you have learned about faith and works in James 2 by playing "Where Am I?"

Look at the following statements and write down next to each sentence WHERE the verse is located.

verse ____ Do not hold your *faith* with an attitude of personal favoritism.

verse ____ God chose the poor to be rich in *faith*.

verse ____ What use is it if someone has *faith* but has no *works*? Can that *faith* save him?

verse ____ "*Faith*, if it has no works, is dead, being by itself."

verse ____ "You have *faith* and I have works; show me your *faith* without the works, and I will show you my *faith* by my works."

verse ____ "*Faith* without *works* is useless."

verse ____ Abraham was justified by *works* when he offered up Isaac his son on the altar.

verse ____ "*Faith* was working with his *works*, and as a result of the works, *faith* was perfected."

verse ____ "You see that a man is justified by works and not by *faith* alone."

verse _____ Rahab the harlot was justified by *works* when she received the messengers and sent them out another way.

verse _____ *"Faith* without works is dead."

Now answer some questions.

Are you fulfilling the royal law?

_____

Look at verses 15 and 16. When you see or hear about people who have a need, do you help? HOW? Tell one way you helped someone this week.

_____

_____

_____

Is your faith like that of the demons? They know who God is, but it doesn't change the way they believe or whom they follow—the devil! Or do you have a faith that works?

_____

Give an example of HOW people can tell your faith is real by what they see.

_____

Great job!

EViDENCE OF MY FAiTH

Wow! It has been a great week! Did you memorize your memory verse? James 2 shows us what real faith is. Let's review all that we have learned about faith this week by matching the statements in the column on the left to the correct statement on the right. Connect them with lines.

Royal law	shows a faith that is real
If you show partiality	to be rich in faith
Real faith	love your neighbor as yourself
God chose the poor	has works
Faith without works	you are committing sin
Helping brother in need	is useless

Way to go!

4

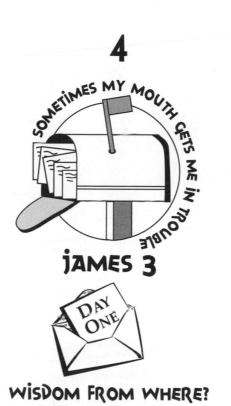

SOMETIMES MY MOUTH GETS ME IN TROUBLE

JAMES 3

DAY ONE

WISDOM FROM WHERE?

Dear Ellie,

I got a letter from someone with a message written in code. The person said this message is for me. My tongue gets me in trouble. I speak too quickly and say things I shouldn't say and don't really mean. This person said I need wisdom from above.

Here's the secret message:

___ ___ ___   ___ ___ ___   ___ ___ ___ ___ ___ ___   ___ ___ ___ ___
2 21 20   20 8 5   23 9 19 4 15 13   6 18 15 13

___ ___ ___ ___ ___   ___ ___   ___ ___ ___ ___ ___ ___   ___ ___ ___ ___ ___,
1 2 15 22 5   9 19   6 9 18 19 20   16 21 18 5

___ ___ ___ ___   ___ ___ ___ ___ ___ ___ ___ ___ ___,
20 8 5 14   16 5 1 3 5 1 2 12 5

___ ___ ___ ___ ___ ___, ___ ___ ___ ___ ___ ___ ___ ___ ___ ___,
7 5 14 20 12 5   18 5 1 19 15 14 1 2 12 5

___ ___ ___ ___ ___ ___   ___ ___ ___ ___ ___ ___   ___ ___ ___   ___ ___ ___ ___
6 21 12 12 15 6   13 5 18 3 25   1 14 4   7 15 15 4

___ ___ ___ ___ ___ ___, ___ ___ ___ ___ ___ ___ ___ ___ ___ ___,
6 18 21 9 20 19   21 14 23 1 22 5 18 9 14 7

___ ___ ___ ___ ___ ___ ___   ___ ___ ___ ___ ___ ___ ___ ___ ___.
23 9 20 8 15 21 20   8 25 16 15 3 18 9 19 25

They said this message is in the Bible in the third chapter of James. What verse is it? I need to memorize it. Can you help me?

Quick Tongue

Why don't you decode Quick Tongue's (QT) message? Here's the secret code.

A B C D E F G H I J K L M N O P Q
1 2 3 4 5 6 7 8 9 10 11 12 13 14 15 16 17

R S T U V W X Y Z
18 19 20 21 22 23 24 25 26

Read James 3. Did you find the verse for the message? Good. Now write QT and give him the verse.

Dear Quick Tongue,

Did you figure out the coded message? It's a great verse—I'm going to memorize this verse with you this week. Why don't you write it on an index card and practice saying it three times a day?

I'll be practicing with you!

_____

STicKS AND STONES...

Let's begin today by choosing another letter from Ellie's desk.

Dear Ellie,

Yesterday at practice one of the girls told me that I am not good enough to be on the cheerleading squad. She said that I look stupid and awkward. I know I am not supposed to let what others say hurt me, but her words really hurt my feelings. Can you help me?

Signed,

Hurt Feelings

Have you ever heard that rhyme "sticks and stones may break my bones, but words will never hurt me"? Now we know that this just isn't true. Words do hurt us. We have all been hurt by something that someone has said to us or about us. What does God have to say about our words? Let's turn to page 133 and take a look at what James 3 says by marking our key words.

tongue, it, says, and *mouth* (mark all the same way with a red tongue)

wise (colored yellow, underlined in orange)

Way to go! Tomorrow we will do more on the tongue.

PUT THAT FIRE OUT!

You did some great research yesterday! Let's ask God for wisdom to teach us about our tongues and how we should use them.

Turn to page 133 and read James 3. See if you can solve today's crossword puzzle about the tongue.

Across

2. James 3:8 The tongue is a restless evil and full of deadly
   _____.

4. James 3:9 WHAT do we do with our tongue to men?
   We _____ men.

5. James 3:6 The tongue is set among our members as that
   which _____ the entire body, and sets on
   fire the course of our life, and is set on fire by hell.

6. James 3:2 If anyone does not stumble in what he
   _____, he is a perfect man, able to bridle the whole
   body as well.

8. James 3:3 We put a bit WHERE on a horse to make it
   obey us? _____

10. James 3:6 The tongue is a _____, the very world
    of iniquity.

Down

1. James 3:5 The tongue is a small part of the body that
   _____ of great things.

3. James 3:9 We use our tongue to do WHAT to our Lord
   and Father? _____

7. James 3:10 From the _____ mouth come
   both blessing and cursing.

9. James 3:8 But no one can _____ the tongue.

BITTER OR SWEET?

James has a lot to say about the tongue, doesn't he?

Let's look for some comparisons about the tongue in our study today. A *comparison* is when you look at how things are alike. A hint that sometimes helps you see a comparison are the words *like* and *as* in the verses you are studying. Here is an example of a comparison: I swim like a fish. How do fish swim? They glide through the water. So if I compare my swimming to that of a fish, then you can be sure I must be a great swimmer. God uses comparisons in His Word to teach us more about our subject. When we study inductively, we need to be on the lookout for comparisons.

Take a look back at James 1:26 on page 130.

What does James mean when he says we are to bridle our tongue?

_____

Let's look at James 3 on page 133 and read verses 1 through 6.

In verse 2 we see if a man has control over what he says, he is able to bridle his body. Let's look for the comparison in verse 3. WHAT controls the horse's body?

_____

Have you ever ridden a horse? HOW do you control the horse? You use a bridle and a bit. A bridle is a harness that fits on the horse's head with a bit that fits inside the horse's mouth over the horse's tongue. The rider holds the reins which are attached to the bit. When the rider pulls on the reins, it puts pressure inside the horse's mouth. This gives the rider control over the whole horse. Just by gently tugging on the reins, a rider can control his horse. That's why James tells us to bridle our tongue. Control over our tongue controls our behavior. The evidence of a faith that is real is having control over our tongue.

Look at James 3:2. Do we ever stumble or are we always perfect?

_____

In James 3:4 we have another comparison to the tongue controlling the body. WHAT is that comparison? (Hint: How is a ship directed?)

_____

James 3:5 With WHAT does James compare a tongue that is out of control?

_____

Read James 3:7-12.

Take two glasses and fill them both with water. The opening of the glass is a picture of our mouth. Now add vinegar to the first glass and sugar to the other. Take a drink from both glasses. WHAT kind of water is poured out of the mouth of the first glass—bitter or sweet?

_____

In James 3:9-10 WHAT comes out of our mouths?

_____

James 3:11 WHAT two kinds of water is James talking about coming from the same fountain?

_____

James 3:12 Can a fig tree produce olives as well as figs?

_____

Can salt water produce fresh water? _____

What two things can our mouths produce?

b _ _ _ _ i n g   c _ _ _ i n g

As Christians, our mouths should always produce what?

_____

Let's look at some cross-references about the tongue.

Proverbs 12:25 WHAT makes a heart glad?

_____

Proverbs 18:21 WHAT is in the power of the tongue?

_____

Proverbs 12:18 WHAT does the tongue of the wise bring?

_____

Let's look at one more cross-reference before we close for the day to see what is said about trees and their fruit.

Look up Luke 6:43-45.

Luke 6:43 WHAT do good trees produce?

_____

WHAT about bad trees?

_____

Luke 6:44 A tree is known by its WHAT?

_____

Luke 6:45 A man speaks from that which fills his

_____.

Whew! We've learned a lot about how our tongue shows what is in our heart. Before we close today, ask yourself these questions:

Do I control my tongue? Or do I yell when I get angry and talk hatefully?

_____

Does my tongue wound by cutting people down or heal by making people feel better? Do I tell my friends how well they did or do I put them down?

_____

Do I need to clean up my bitter water and make it sweet?

_____

What kind of fruit am I producing?

_____

Now go to the Lord and ask forgiveness if you have stumbled. Ask Him to give you good fruit that shows other people that you have a faith that is real.

WHEN YOU THINK YOU'RE SO SMART!

Today we need to finish our study of James 3 so that we can answer Hurt Feelings's letter.

Turn to James 3 on page 133.

Yesterday we learned how to find comparisons. Today let's look at *contrasts*. Contrasts show how two things are different or opposite. An example of a contrast would be *light* and *dark*.

Now that we know what contrasts are, let's contrast *wisdom from above* to *wisdom that does not come from above* in James 3:13-17. Read these verses and list the words that describe the differences in wisdom from above and wisdom not from above.

Wisdom from Above   Wisdom Not from Above

_____   _____

_____   _____

_____   _____

_____   _____

_____   _____

_____   _____

_____

James 3:13 HOW do we show our good behavior?

_____

James 3:18 If you sow peace, WHAT is your fruit?

_____

Do you know what righteousness is? It is God's gift to those who believe on the Lord Jesus Christ and are brought into a right relationship with God. It is a gift that cannot be earned. It is all that God requires a person to be, but it's what a person could never do on his or her own.

Turn to Psalm 119:23-24 to see what we are to do when someone hurts us with words.

Even though princes _____ and _____ against me,

Your servant _____ on Your _____.

Your testimonies also are my _____; they are my

_____.

Before you answer Hurt Feelings ask yourself, these questions.

Is your wisdom from above?_____

When your friends pick on someone by making fun of his or her size, nose, ears, or something else, do you join them? Or do you stand up for the person being made fun of?

_____

Are you jealous of your best friend because she made all A's, or are you happy and excited for her?

_____

Do you try to get along with everyone? Or do you tell one friend what another friend said about him in order to make them mad or start a fight?

_____

Now take everything you've learned this week and answer Hurt Feelings's letter.

Dear Hurt Feelings,

_I am so sorry to hear that one of the girls said such an ugly and hurtful thing to you. I have been studying James 3 this week, and I have learned a lot about the tongue and how we are to use it. First I saw in James 1:26 that I am to _____ my tongue to show that my faith is real. I also saw in James 3:2 that we all _____. But our tongue is not to be out of control. Both _____ and cursing should not come out of our mouths. We are to have a _____ that is from above that is _____, _____, gentle, reasonable, full of mercy and good fruits, unwavering, and without hypocrisy. Then we will bring peace and not conflict. We will show other people our faith is genuine when what comes out of our mouths demonstrates that God is living inside us. I am so sorry that this girl used her tongue to wound you. Let God use this trial to help you think about how you speak to others. You can't control other girls' tongues, but you can control yours! Do you make fun of others? Have you talked disrespectfully to your parents?_

Have you ever used bad words? If you have ever stumbled, then go to the Lord and ask Him for forgiveness. God loves us. He hurts when we hurt. Turn to Him when someone hurts your feelings, and let Him heal your heart.

Praying for you,

_____

Congratulations on all that you have learned! Remember: Be a doer of the Word and not just a hearer!

P.S. Here's an experiment to remind us to be slow to speak and to watch our words and make sure they are sweet. Get a tube of toothpaste from the grocery store and a piece of paper. Now squeeze the toothpaste tube and write the words "love" and "hate" with toothpaste. See how easy it is to get the words to come out of the tube? Now try putting those "words" back inside the tube. Can you do it? Will those words go back inside once they have been squeezed out? This is a reminder of how easy it is to say things and how hard it is, once we've spoken, to take back what we've said. We need to make sure our words are sweet and not hurtful to other people.

5

SOMETIMES ALL i THINK ABOUT iS ME

JAMES 4

SIN

Mr. Chase talked to Ellie this morning, and Ellie is feeling much better. She is so proud of all your hard work and can't wait to read your column this week.

Let's start today with our memory verse for this week. It's James 4:17, the last verse in chapter 4, and it deals with sin. Fill in the blanks of your verse below and practice saying it three times today.

James 4:17 Therefore, to _____ who _____the

_____ thing to do and _____ _____ do it, to

him it is _____.

Now see if you can find all the words in your verse by circling them in this word search.

```
E R O F E R E H T
K O I S E O D O H
N H S G E N O R I
O W I T H E T O N
W A N D I T H E G
S H I M T T U A J
```

AND	WHO
DO	NOT
DOES	ONE
HIM	RIGHT
IS	SIN
IT	THE
KNOWS	THEREFORE
TO	THING

Now, in your own words, give an example of what this verse means using your own experience or a friend's experience. Ask your Mom or Dad to help you if you can't think of one.

_____

_____

_____

MINE, MINE, MINE

You did a great job yesterday! Today we will begin our research on James 4. Have you prayed and practiced your memory verse? If so, let's get started by opening another letter to Ellie.

Dear Ellie,

My two friends are always fighting and dragging me into the middle of their fight. I like both of them and do not want to be put in the middle. They are so jealous of each other. If one of them gets something, the other one has to have it, too. I do not understand why both of these friends who say they are Christians fight and tear each other down all the time. Can you help me?

Signed,

Stuck in the Middle

It seems like Stuck in the Middle has quite a problem. His two friends that he cares about say they are Christians, and yet they can't get along. Let's turn to James 4 on page 134 and see what the Bible has to say about fighting and quarreling.

Read James 4:1-10.

James 4:1 WHAT is James' first question to the Jewish believers?

_____

_____

James 4:1 WHAT does James say is the source that wages war in your members?

_____

James 4:2 WHAT causes people to commit murder?

_____

James does not mean literal murder here, but anger and hating one another.

Pleasures are things you do to please yourself, to get what you desire. Lust means you desire something—you want what someone else has.

James 4:2 WHAT causes fighting and quarreling?

_____

What does it mean to be envious? It means you are unhappy when you think of what someone else has. It is a strong desire to have for yourself what that person has (such as a friend getting a new bike—the very one you have always wanted, but it was too expensive for you to buy).

Is the problem of envy inside the person or outside the person?

_____

We see that the root of this problem is our pleasures, our lust, and our envying. These problems come from within us, not from without. Let's look a little farther.

James 4:2-3 WHY do these persons not have something? WHAT is the reason James gives us?

_____

WHY do you think they are not praying?

_____

_____

James 4:3 WHAT are their wrong motives?

_____

Let's turn to Philippians 4:19. WHO is to supply our needs?

_____

Just some of our needs or all of them?

_____

Great job! Have you learned a lot today? Tomorrow we will come back to this subject. Before we close for the day, we want you to think about what you have studied.

Many times the reason we do not get along is because we are jealous of what each other has and sometimes of the way we look. We are only thinking about ourselves and what we want (our pleasures).

Who is the Giver of our needs? Who made us in His image? Do we have the right to be jealous over what our friends have that we do not have? Where does every good thing come from?

Read James 1:17. Thank God for what you have. And remember, if God doesn't give us something, it's because He doesn't think it is good for us, we have asked for it with the wrong motive, or it isn't the right time.

Why don't you look inside your heart for any jealousy or envy that causes problems with your friends? Write a short prayer to God asking for His help and thanking Him for hearing your prayers. Remember your memory verse: "Therefore, to one who knows the right thing to do and does not do it, to him it is sin."

_____

_____

_____

_____

FRIEND OF GOD OR FRIEND OF THE WORLD?

Yesterday was a tough lesson, wasn't it? God uses His Word to show us when we sin, as well as how we are to live. Sometimes it can be painful to see why we are having problems. But isn't it great that God loves us so much that He wants His very best for us? Today we are going to continue in James 4. Turn to pages 134-135 and read James 4:1-10.

James 4:4 WHAT is friendship with the world?

_____

Look up *hostility* in a dictionary. WHAT does it mean?

_____

James 4:4 WHAT do you make yourself when you are a friend of the world?

_____

Let's talk about worldliness. Is worldliness how we dress, what we eat, or what we listen to? Is it what we do on the outside, or is it what we are on the inside?

Worldliness is a focus on self. It is selfish and self-centered. It's *Me, Me, Me,* and *Mine, Mine, Mine!* It is a self-centered, not God-centered, attitude.

Look up John 15:18. WHOM does the world hate?

_____

(If you've used the *Jesus, Awesome Power, Awesome Love* workbook, you've already studied this! Wasn't it great? Do you see how Scripture helps us understand Scripture?)

The world hates Jesus, therefore we are not to love the world or be friends with it. The world wants our attention to be on ourselves. God wants our total loyalty and devotion to be to Him.

James 4:5,6 To WHOM does God give greater grace?

_____

Are you proud or are you humble? Do you want what you want or what God wants? Finish the sentence:

I _____

WHAT are our instructions then? HOW are we to be humble? James 4:7-10 gives us ten things we are to do to be God-centered and not self-centered. WHAT are those ten things?

1. James 4:7 _____

2. James 4:7 _____

3. James 4:8 _____

4. James 4:8 _____

5. James 4:8 _____

6. James 4:9 _____

7. James 4:9 _____

8. James 4:9 _____

9. James 4:9 _____

10. James 4:10 _____

Now why don't you write Stuck in the Middle and share with him what you've learned about fighting and worldliness?

Dear Stuck in the Middle,

I was so sorry to hear about your two friends fighting all the time. I know how hard it must be for you since they are both your friends. I have been studying James 4. He says fighting and quarreling happen because of wanting the things we do not have, whether it is the way we look or things that we own. We fight and quarrel because we are self-centered and seek to please ourselves. This makes us friends with the world and an _____ of _____. James tells us we do not _____, so we do not have, or we ask with _____ _____. God's desire is that we put Him first. We are to humble ourselves and give our devotion to Him, not to me, me, me. He gives us ten instructions in James 4:7-10 on how to do this. Maybe you can share these with your two friends and show them how their jealousy is the cause of their fights. I will be praying for you and that God will open your friends' eyes to the way they are behaving.

Trusting in Him,

_____

You are doing great!

jUDGe NOT!

Yesterday we looked at how to humble ourselves. Let's turn to James 4 on pages 134-135 and read James 4:11-17.
Now let's mark our key words.

judge (draw a brown judge's gavel)

speak against (since we speak with our mouth, let's mark this with a *red tongue*).

James 4:11 WHAT are we *not* to do to our brother?

_____

If you speak against your brother, WHAT are you doing

to your brother? _____ him.

If you are speaking against and therefore judging your brother, WHAT are you doing to the law?

_____

If you _____ the law, you are not a _____

of the law but a _____ of it.

Are we to judge the law? Read James 4:12. James tells us there are HOW many judges and lawgivers?

_____

WHO is that Judge and Lawgiver?

_____

Do you remember the royal law in James 2:8? Write it out below.

You shall _____ your _____ as

_____.

Read James 2:13. WHAT will God's judgment be like to you if you have shown no mercy?

_____

Mercy is having pity and compassion toward the person who needs it. It is being kind and forgiving to an enemy. It is God's compassion for us when we are in distress.

God shows us very clearly in James that we are not to judge our brother. We are to love our brother. This doesn't mean we can't judge a brother's wrong behavior. His behavior needs to be right according to God's Word. We need to tell our brother when his behavior is wrong. We don't judge the person—just the behavior. Our responsibility as Christians is to be doers of the Word, showing love and mercy to each other, not judgment.

James 4:13 WHAT are the people doing in this verse?

_____

James 4:14 WHAT is our life compared to in this verse?

_____

Do we know what our life will be like tomorrow?

_____

James 4:15 WHAT should we do instead?

_____

James 4:16 By making plans of our own instead of seeking God's plan for us, WHAT are we doing?

_____

What is arrogance? Look it up in your dictionary.

_____

James 4:16 says this boasting is WHAT?

_____

Does this please God?

_____

No! Our arrogance and pride never please God. When we focus on what we want to do and what we want instead of seeking God's plan for us, we are putting ourselves in God's place. We are walking independently from Him. God wants our total love and devotion. He wants us to bow before Him and let Him have His way with our lives. We need to ask God what His plan is for us.

Are you guilty of judging and speaking against other people? Do you make your plans without asking God what you should do? If so, confess to God that you have spoken against other people and have done things your way instead of asking God what His plan is for you. Ask God to help you love your brother by showing mercy instead of judgment. And ask Him to show you what His plans are for you.

Go to your sister or brother or a friend that you have criticized (either to his face or behind his back) and practice the royal law by saying something positive to him instead of a criticism. You can do it. If you are a Christian, God's Spirit lives in you! Remember: He "who knows the right thing to do and does not do it, to him it is sin."

After you do it write down what happened or how you feel. God will be so pleased by your obedience.

_____

_____

_____

LET'S TALK ABOUT SIN

Whew! James has some hard lessons for us, but what a wonderful book that gives practical help for all our problems. And doesn't it feel good when we do what pleases God? Let's turn to James 4 on page 135 one more time and look at verse 17, our memory verse for the week.

James 4:17 WHAT are we doing if we know the right thing to do and we don't do it?

_____

Let's go back in James and mark this key word in each chapter of James where it shows up:

sin (colored brown)—James 1:15; James 2:9; James 2:11 (mark *transgressor of the law* the same as *sin*)

Now let's have a place in our notebook that tells us what God calls sin.

What God Calls Sin

James 1:13-15 _____

James 2:9-11 _____

James 4:17 _____

WHAT do we learn about sin? WHAT does sin bring forth? (James 1:15)

_____

WHO died for our sins?

_____

God paid a huge price for sin. It cost Him His one and only Son, Jesus. In light of this, should we ever take sin lightly? If our faith is real, we will not take sin lightly. We will examine ourselves and humble ourselves before the Lord.

What a great week! You did a lot of studying and a great job of helping Stuck in the Middle with his problem.

Why don't you try and write your memory verse below without looking it up?

_____

_____

_____

We are so excited about all you have learned!

6

SOMETIMES RICH PEOPLE BOTHER ME

JAMES 5:1-12

WARNINGS!

Today we start in the last chapter of James. Let's begin by looking at our secret coded memory verse for this week. Break the code and practice saying your verse three times today.

The Code												
A	B	C	D	E	F	G	H	I	J	K	L	M
1	2	3	4	5	6	7	8	9	10	11	12	13
N	O	P	Q	R	S	T	U	V	W	X	Y	Z
14	15	16	17	18	19	20	21	22	23	24	25	26

__ __ __ __ __ __ __ __ __ __ __ __ __ ʼ
4 15   14 15 20   3 15 13 16 12 1 9 14

__ __ __ __ __ __ __ __ ʼ __ __ __ __ __ __ __ __ __ __ __
2 18 5 20 8 18 5 14   1 7 1 9 14 19 20   15 14 5

__ __ __ __ __ __ __, __ __ __ __ __ __ __ __ __
1 14 15 20 8 5 18   19 15   20 8 1 20 25 15 21

__ __ __ __ __ __ __ __ __ __ __ __ __ __ __ __ __ __
25 15 21 18 19 5 12 22 5 19   13 1 25   14 15 20   2 5

__ __ __ __ __ __; __ __ __ __ __ __; __ __ __
10 21 4 7 5 4   2 5 8 15 12 4   20 8 5

__ __ __ __ __ __ __ __ __ __ __ __ __ __ __
10 21 4 7 5   9 19   19 20 1 14 4 9 14 7

__ __ __ __ __ __ __ __ __ __ __ __ __ __.
18 9 7 8 20   1 20   20 8 5   4 15 15 18

Now let's turn to James 5 on page 136 and look at our Observation Worksheet. Read James 5:1-12. It contains our secret coded memory verse. Then mark the following key words. *Don't forget to mark your pronouns!*

rich (green $—watch for *you* when it refers to the rich and mark it the same way)

last days (green clock)

coming of the Lord (draw a purple cloud, color it blue and yellow)

<u>be patient</u> (red underline)

Judged (brown judge's gavel)

Way to go! Tomorrow we will begin to take a closer look at these key words.

THE WICKED RICH

The mail boy has just brought in a new bag of mail. Let's read a letter from Treated Unfairly before we get started.

Dear Ellie,

I am a Christian, and I try to treat everyone the way Jesus tells us to in the Bible. Why does it seem like it doesn't matter how I behave? Some of the rich kids in our school are selfish and mean. They always seem to get everything their way. Life just doesn't seem to be fair. The rich come out on top regardless of their behavior. What does God have to say about the rich who don't love Him?

Signed,

Treated Unfairly

What a question! We know James has talked a lot about the rich, so let's look at James 5 on page 136 where we began our observations yesterday.

Read James 5:1-6. Let's find out to WHOM James is talking and WHAT he has to say?

James 5:1 To WHOM is James talking?

_____

Does he call these rich his brethren?

_____

James 5:1 WHAT does James tell the rich to do?

_____

WHY? _____

_____

James 5:2-3 List WHAT has happened to their riches.

riches   _____

garments   _____

gold and silver   _____

From what has happened to the rich man's possessions, do riches last?

_____

James 5:3 WHAT have the rich done in the last days?

_____

Since we have seen that riches do not last, should we store up riches for ourselves?

_____

James 5:4 HOW did the rich treat the laborers who worked for them?

_____

James 5:5 HOW did the rich live on the earth?

_____

James 5:6 WHAT did the rich do to the righteous man?

_____

Wow! James really gives it to the rich—telling them to weep and howl. And no wonder! Look at how they have lived and treated others. From what you have learned about these rich people, are they Christians?

_____

No! That's why James does not address them as brethren (the Jewish Christians he has been writing to). But these rich do not include all rich people. These are the wicked rich who are not Christians.

WHY do you think James puts this warning about the wicked rich in his letter to the brethren?

_____

Let's read Psalm 73:1-3.

Psalm 73:2 WHAT happens to the psalmist's feet?

_____

Psalm 73:3 WHY did his feet come close to slipping?

_____

_____

The psalmist sounds a lot like Treated Unfairly. He sees the wicked prospering, and his feet almost stumble. James' warning to the rich is to be an encouragement to the brethren. The wicked rich people have their misery coming.

Read James 5:3-5. WHAT lesson can you apply to

your life?_____

_____

Where do you fall on a scale of 1 to 10? Circle the number that best shows where you are. Ten is the best and one is the worst.

Are you content with what you have?

_____

1	2	3	4	5	6	7	8	9	10

not content   a little content   very content

Is your mind focused on getting more things?

_____

1	2	3	4	5	6	7	8	9	10

yes (more, more, more)   a little more   no (I'm satisfied)

Are you disappointed at Christmas if your friends get more things than you get?

_____

1	2	3	4	5	6	7	8	9	10

very disappointed   a little disappointed   not disappointed

Do you ask your parents for more than they can afford?

1	2	3	4	5	6	7	8	9	10
all the time				sometimes				very seldom	

How do you act when you don't get what you want?

1	2	3	4	5	6	7	8	9	10
get very angry			beg and plead			accept parents' decision			

Do you ever do extra work to earn money to buy things you need so that your parents don't have to?

1	2	3	4	5	6	7	8	9	10
never				sometimes				very often	

How many video games do you have?

1	2	3	4	5	6	7	8	9	10
not enough			I could use a few more				enough		

Why don't you go to the Lord and ask Him to help you be careful in how you treat possessions?

Do you live a life of pleasure, thinking only of what you can get?

Is there someone you could help by selling some of your possessions or by giving some away?

Now look at the warning in 1 Timothy 6:9-10 printed below. Mark the words *rich, it,* and *money* with a green $.

1 Timothy 6:9-11

Verse 9 But those who want to get rich fall into temptation and a snare and many foolish and harmful desires which plunge men into ruin and destruction.

Verse 10 For the love of money is a root of all sorts of evil, and some by longing for it have wandered away from the faith and pierced themselves with many griefs.

Verse 11 But flee from these things, you man of God, and pursue righteousness, godliness, faith, love, and perseverance and gentleness.

Write out a brief prayer to God, asking Him to help you not be like the wicked rich, but to live a life that pleases Him.

_____

_____

_____

_____

Great job! We are so proud of you!

THE LAST DAYS

Have you practiced your memory verse for the week? Great! Let's start today by looking at James 5:3.

Use the puzzle below to answer WHEN the rich have stored up their treasure. Begin at the top arrow and go to the bottom arrow in seven moves.

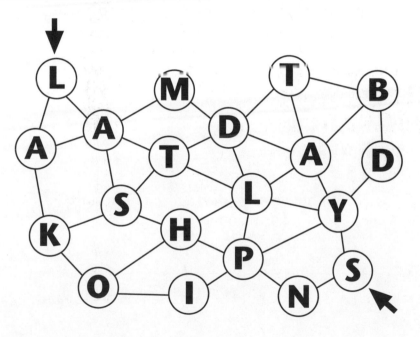

Let's look at some cross-references to help us understand what James means by "the last days."

Look up Hebrews 1:1-2.
In the last days God has spoken to us HOW?

_____

Let's look at 2 Peter 3:3-4.
WHAT happens in the last days?

_____

WHAT event are the mockers talking about?

_____

   We see in Hebrews that the last days begin with Jesus' first coming to earth. We see in 2 Peter that in the last days mockers are asking where is the promise of Jesus' coming. Did you know that Jesus is coming again? If the last days began when Jesus came the first time, we know that we are living in the last days according to God.

   In 2 Peter 3:8-9 HOW long is a day to the Lord?

_____

WHAT year is it now? _____

Then about how many "days" has it been since Jesus came if He was born around 4 B.C.?

_____

Is the Lord slow about His promise (to come again)?

_____

WHY is the Lord patiently waiting?

_____

   Isn't that awesome? God loves us so much that He is patient toward us, not wanting any of us to perish, but for all of us to come to repentance. Repentance means to change our minds and believe Jesus is God and receive Him as our Lord. When we do this, we become God's children. So we had better get busy and share this good news so people will believe and Jesus will return.

Tomorrow we will study more about Jesus coming again and what James has to say about it. Hang in there!

BE PATiENT!

Are you ready to do some more studying on the coming of the Lord? Isn't this exciting? Jesus is someday going to be King over all the earth! Don't forget to ask God to help you understand what His Word has to say. Now let's turn to page 136 and read James 5:7-11.

James is no longer warning the wicked rich in verse 7. To WHOM is James talking?

_____

WHAT is he telling the brethren to do?

_____

James 5:7 HOW long are they to be patient?

_____

WHAT example of patience does James gives the believers in verse 7?

_____

James 5:8 Besides being patient, WHAT else is the

believer to do?_____

WHY? _____

Let's take a minute and do some cross-referencing. Look
at John 14:1-4. In John 14:2, Jesus goes WHERE?

_____

John 14:3 If Jesus goes and prepares a place for us, what
else is He going to do?

_____

Now look at Acts 1:9-12.
Acts 1:11 WHO was taken into heaven?

_____

WHO will come back the same way that He went into
heaven?

_____

So we see from cross-referencing that Jesus is definitely
coming back again. Therefore, we are to be patient and
strengthen our hearts until He comes for us. Go back to James
5, and let's see what else we learn.

James 5:9 WHAT are we not to do to one another?

_____

WHY? _____

WHO is standing at the door? _____

That means it won't be too long before Jesus comes again!

Jesus came to the earth the first time as a baby. He became a human being just like us, but without sin. God was His Father. Mary was His earthly mother. He came as our Savior to save us from our sins. The next time He comes, it will be as a Judge. The Judge is standing at the door.

Let's do a little more cross-referencing and see what else the Bible has to say about Jesus as the Judge.

Read Revelation 19:10-16.

These verses are about Jesus coming again, just like James says. Color or mark every reference to Jesus like this _____ in purple, including the pronouns *He* and *His* and synonyms like *Faithful, True,* and *Word of God*. Then color it yellow.

Revelation 19:10-16

Verse 10 Then I fell at his feet to worship him. But he said to me, "Do not do that; I am a fellow servant of yours and your brethren who hold the testimony of Jesus; worship God. For the testimony of Jesus is the spirit of prophecy."

Verse 11 And I saw heaven opened, and behold, a white horse, and He who sat on it is called Faithful and True, and in righteousness He judges and wages war.

Verse 12 His eyes are a flame of fire, and on His head are many diadems, and He has a name written on Him which no one knows except Himself.

Verse 13 He is clothed with a robe dipped in blood, and His name is called The Word of God.

Verse 14 And the armies which are in heaven, clothed in fine linen, white and clean, were following Him on white horses.

Verse 15 From His mouth comes a sharp sword, so that with it He may strike down the nations, and He will rule them with a rod of iron; and He treads the wine press of the fierce wrath of God, the Almighty.

Verse 16 And on His robe and on His thigh He has a name written, "King of kings, and Lord of lords."

Draw a picture below of Jesus as He is pictured in these verses.

In James 4:12 we saw there is only one Lawgiver and Judge—the One who is able to save and destroy. Therefore, we are not to judge because there is a Judge coming who will do the judging. We are to be patient and let Jesus be the Judge. Jesus can judge us because He became a man—a human being just like us—but He never sinned.

Christians will be judged at the judgment seat of Christ (Romans 14:10; 2 Corinthians 5:10) and given their reward. Non-Christians will be judged at the great white throne judgment according to their deeds and thrown into the lake of fire (Revelation 20:11-15).

We saw yesterday how patient God is about Jesus' second coming, and now we see why. God loves us so much that He wants us in heaven with Him. So He is waiting for all to be saved so that we will not perish in the lake of fire.

Let's go back to James 5:10-11.

James 5:10 WHO is to be our example of suffering and patience?

_____

James 5:11 WHAT words describe those who endured?

_____

James 5:11 WHO is our example of endurance?

_____

James 5:11 WHAT do we see about the Lord in this verse?

_____

WHO IS JOB?

Job was a man who was blameless, upright, feared God, and turned from evil. Yet God put him through many trials, and he suffered greatly. Job did not sin with his lips. He trusted God and endured whatever hardship the Lord gave him. In the end he was greatly blessed. Job is a wonderful example of how God allows Christians to be tested so He can prove their faith is real.

You did a great job! I know God is pleased with all your hard work today. I think you are ready to answer Treated Unfairly's letter.

Dear Treated Unfairly,

You are right—life is not fair! But God's Word holds the answers to our problems. I have been studying James 5 this week, and he has a lot to say about the rich who do not love the Lord. James warns them to _____ and _____ because their _____ are coming upon them. Their riches have _____ and their garments are _____-_____ and their gold and silver have _____. What do you think about that? The rich who don't know Jesus may prosper, but their time is coming. In James 5:7, he tells us to _____ _____ until the _____ of the _____. We are not to complain against one another so that we may not be _____, because the _____ is standing at the door. As Christians we are to be patient, to strengthen our hearts, and to endure suffering. We have seen

through the trials of Job that the Lord is full of
_____ *and is merciful. You have a com-*
passionate Father who cares about you and will
judge those who treat you wrongly when He comes
again. I hope that this encourages you not to stum-
ble but to keep living the way God tells you in His
Word. That way other people can see a faith that is
real. I will be praying for you.

Until Jesus comes,

_____

Why don't you close by thanking God that Jesus is coming soon? Remember: Be patient!

LET YOUR YES BE YES!

Ellie loved the letter you wrote to Treated Unfairly yesterday! She is so proud of all your hard work to help other people.

Let's turn to James 5:12 on page 135. Here we go again with our tongue and what we are to say.

James 5:12 WHAT are the brethren not to do?

_____

HOW?_____

WHY? _____

Once again James is warning us to be careful with our tongue. As Christians we are to be careful that we do not use God's name in a careless way which does not treat Him as the holy God that He is. To violate God's name is to violate God.

We are not to use God's name in an oath to guarantee our truthfulness (like swearing that you are telling the truth or hope to die). Do not swear! You are to be consistent in always telling the truth so that you don't have to cross your heart and hope to die. Just do the good things that you say you will do. Let your yes always be yes and your no always be no, and nothing else will be needed.

Are you careful with your speech?

_____

Have you used the Lord's name to swear by?

_____

If so, then go to God and confess your sin so that you will not fall under judgment. Ask God to help you watch what you say and how you say it.

You did a great job this week! Did you learn your memory verse? Remember: Don't complain against one another. Be united. The Lord is coming!

7

JAMES 5:13-20

WHAT TO DO?

Are you ready to do your last Observation Worksheet in the book of James? Then let's turn to page 136 and read James 5:13-20. Let's mark our final key words for this book.

pray, prayer, and prayed (colored pink)

sins (brown)

Now fill in the blanks for your memory verse, James 5:16, and practice saying it.

Therefore, _____ your _____ to one another,

and pray for one another so that _____ may be

_____. The effective _____ of a

_____ man can _____ much.

Way to go! See you tomorrow.

DEAR ELLIE. . .

Let's go to Ellie's desk one more time. Here's a letter from a new believer about prayer.

> Dear Ellie,
>
> I have been reading your column. I am a new Christian, and I have some questions about praying. When should we pray, and how do we pray? I hope you can help me because I want to do what God wants me to do.
>
> Signed,
>
> New Believer

Isn't that wonderful? A new believer!

Let's thank God for our new brother or sister in Christ.

Now, let's go to page 136 and read James 5:13-18. Solve the following crossword puzzle.

Across

1. James 5:15 The Lord will raise him up, and if he has committed sins, they will be _____ him.

3. James 5:14 The elders are to pray over him and anoint him with _____.

4. James 5:14 The _____ person must call for the elders of the church to pray over him.

6. James 5:13 When you are cheerful, you are to sing_____.

8. James 5:15 The prayer offered in faith will _____ the one who is sick.

9. James 5:16 Pray for one another so that you may be _____.

Down

1. James 5:17 Who prayed earnestly that it would not rain?_____

2. James 5:16 The effective prayer of a _____ man can accomplish much.

5. James 5:16 _____ your sins to one another.

6. James 5:13 Is anyone among you suffering? Then he must _____.

7. James 5:14 He is to be anointed in the name of the _____.

ELiJAH

James uses Elijah as an example. Let's look at Elijah by doing some cross-referencing and find out why.

James 5:17 WHAT kind of man was Elijah?

_____

Look up 1 Kings 19:1-3. This happens after Elijah has a great victory. He has just called on God, and God sent down fire from heaven and burned up a sacrifice that was soaking wet. But now WHAT does 1 Kings 19:3 tell us about Elijah?

_____

That's pretty ordinary, isn't it?

Going back to James 5:17, HOW did Elijah pray?

_____

WHAT did Elijah pray for?

_____

James 5:18 WHAT did Elijah pray for the second time?

_____

Did God answer Elijah's prayers?

_____

Elijah had gone to King Ahab and told him in 1 Kings 17:1 that it would not rain. How did Elijah—an ordinary guy—have the courage to tell the king it would not rain? Let's find out a little bit about King Ahab. Turn to 1 Kings 16 and read verses 30 through 34.

1 Kings 16:30 WHAT kind of king was Ahab?

_____

Did King Ahab serve other gods?

_____

Turn to Deuteronomy 11:13-17.

WHAT did God say He would give if the Israelites obeyed?

_____

Deuteronomy 11:16-17 If they disobeyed by serving other gods, WHAT would God take away?

_____

Elijah knew God's Word. He was just an ordinary person, like us, who knew what God said would happen if the people disobeyed Him. So when Elijah prayed earnestly, asking God not to send rain, he knew how to pray because he knew his God. He knew God controls even the weather!

How about you? Do you know God?

Studying and knowing His Word will show you how you are to pray in all circumstances.

Let's thank God for giving us His Word so we can know how to pray.

_____

_____

_____

_____

_____

PRAYER AND SIN

Look at all you have learned about prayer so far this week! What effect do you think sin has on a person's prayer life? Let's do some cross-referencing and see what God has to say about sin and prayer.

Read Isaiah 59:1,2 WHAT is the result of sin?
Your iniquities have made a _____ between

_____ and _____ __ _____.

Your sins have_____.

Read Psalm 66:18 WHAT is the result of sin in this verse?

_____

Read Proverbs 28:13 WHAT happens when you conceal your transgressions?

_____

From these verses we see that sin hinders our prayers and our relationship with God. Now let's look at what restores our relationship and our prayer life with God. Looking back at Proverbs 28:13, HOW do you find compassion?

_____

Look up 1 John 1:9. WHAT does this verse say we need to do?

_____

WHAT does God do WHEN we confess our sins?

He _____ our sins and _____

us from all _____.

In James 5:16, WHAT does James tell us to do?

_____

After we confess, WHAT are we to do?

_____

WHAT kind of man can accomplish much with an effective prayer?

_____

Let's make a list of all we have seen about prayer.

When to pray

_____

_____

_____

_____

What to pray for

_____

_____

_____

_____

Results of prayer

_____

_____

_____

_____

Now write a letter to New Believer and share what God has taught you about prayer.

Dear New Believer,

I was so excited to get your letter and know that there is a new member in God's family! I am glad that you wrote asking about prayer. We see in James 1:5 that we are to ____ God for wisdom. James 5:13 tells us God wants us to _____ when we are troubled (suffering), happy, sick, and when we have sinned. We are to call on the _____ of the _____ to pray over us when we are _____. We are to confess our sins to God so that He can cleanse us. We also need to confess to other Christians so they can pray for us. We need to know God's Word so that we can pray His will for our lives. Only God can meet all our needs, heal, and cleanse us from sin. I am so thankful for you and will be lifting you up in prayer that God will continue to teach you how to pray.

Your prayer warrior,

_____

How about you?
Do you pray every day? yes   no (circle one)

What kind of things do you pray about:

_____   _____   _____

_____   _____   _____

Do you thank God for who He is and that He gave you
Jesus? yes   no (circle one)

Do you treat God like "Santa Claus" by constantly asking for things? yes   no (circle one)

Do you ask God for help when you have a problem, like
making a bad grade on a test? Circle the number that
best shows what you do.

| 1 | 2 | 3 | 4 | 5 | 6 | 7 | 8 | 9 | 10 |

never (I can do it myself)   sometimes   always—I need God's help

Do you ask for forgiveness when you have been mean to
your brother or sister? yes   no (circle one)

When a friend is sick, do you ask God to make him
well?

| 1 | 2 | 3 | 4 | 5 | 6 | 7 | 8 | 9 | 10 |

No—he can go to a doctor   sometimes   always

Spend some time thinking about what you have learned
about prayer and about how you pray. Then go to God and
ask Him to teach you to pray in a way that pleases Him.

TURN HIM BACK

Let's look at the last two verses in James. Turn to page 136 to James 5:19-20.

To WHOM is James talking?

_____

James 5:19 WHAT is James' concern?

_____

James 5:19 WHAT does James tell the Christian to do to a brother who strays from the truth?

_____

James 5:20 WHAT are you turning a sinner from?

_____

James 5:20 WHAT are you saving the sinner from?

_____

Once again, James is telling us in these verses to be a doer of the Word. If we have a faith that is real, we will care about other people. We will turn a sinner from the error of his way. We'll help him understand his problems and how to solve them according to the truth, God's Word.

Draw a picture of yourself praying with someone. Then think of someone you know who needs to know the Lord, and pray for that person.

Way to go! We are so proud of you! You have just finished the book of James. Isn't that awesome!

Ellie has a letter just for you, and then we have a fun game for you to play called "Doer of the Word." It will help remind you of all that you've learned by studying the book of James.

A Letter from Ellie

Guess what? Ellie is well and back at her desk. She has written a letter just for you.

Dear_____,

   I am so thankful for you! You did a terrific job answering all my letters while I was out with the flu! Look at all you have learned from studying God's Word for yourself in the book of James. You know what it means to have a faith that is real and how to be a doer of the Word. You have learned that God is in control of everything that happens to us—even the bad things. God uses the bad things to test our faith to see if it is real and to make us perfect and complete. You learned to ask God for wisdom and how to avoid temptation. You learned why to pray, and how to handle anger and your tongue. You know what sin and worldliness are, and that Jesus is coming again! Isn't that exciting to know that Jesus is coming back for us? You also learned about putting others first. (Remember the "royal law"?) I am so proud of you! I hope you'll continue to study God's Word so that you will grow up mature and complete. If you go to www.precept.org/D4Ycertificate you can print a certificate you can frame or put on your bulletin board. We look forward to doing another study with you soon!

   Remember to count it all joy!

   Love,

   Ellie

Now try our "Doer of the Word" game. You can play it by yourself or with a friend or family member.

What you'll need: The game board on the next page, Hearers or Doers cards on the page after that (you'll need to cut these out), a coin to flip, and a marker for each player.

How to play: Place the Hearer or Doer cards facedown in the square provided on the game board. Start with your marker on the Start circle. Flip a coin. Heads, you move two spaces. Tails, you move one space. If you land on a space marked HD (Hearers or Doers), pick up the top card from the pile and follow the instructions. Then return the card to the bottom of the pile. Have fun!

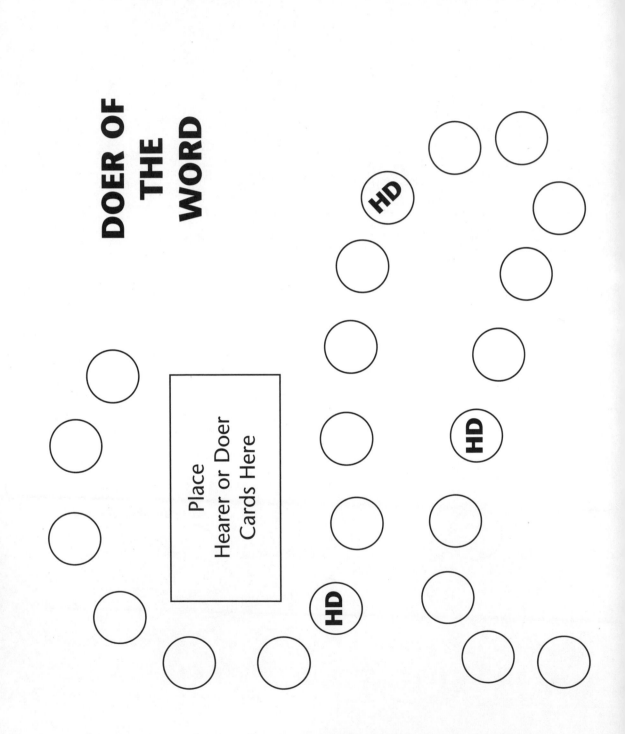

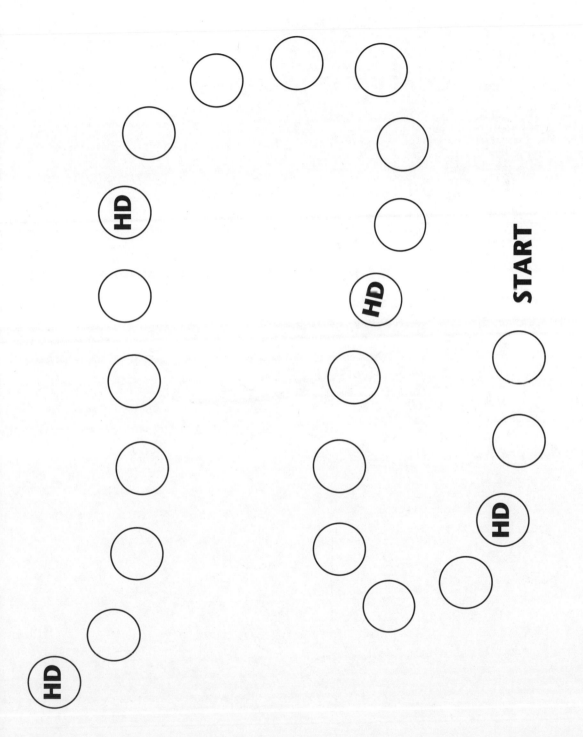

START

HD

HD

HD

HD

GAME PIECES NEXT PAGE

ASK GOD FOR WISDOM Move ahead 3 spaces	MAKE FUN OF SOMEONE'S NAME Go back 2 spaces
BUY A TOY FOR A NEEDY CHILD Move ahead 2 spaces	VISIT A NURSING HOME Move ahead 1 space
LOSE YOUR TEMPER Lose one turn	WATCH A TV SHOW YOU SHOULDN'T HAVE Go back 1 space
COMFORT SOMEONE WHO WAS MADE FUN OF Move ahead 3 spaces	RETURN A LOST WALLET Move ahead 1 space
TALK BACK TO YOUR PARENTS Go back 3 spaces	FIGHT WITH YOUR BEST FRIEND Go back 2 spaces
RECITE JAMES 1:2-4 If you can, move ahead 2 spaces	RECITE JAMES 1:22 If you can, move ahead 2 spaces
RECITE JAMES 2:8 If you can, move ahead 2 spaces	RECITE JAMES 4:17 If you can, move ahead 2 spaces
COMPLIMENT A FRIEND Move ahead 1 space	CAUGHT THE FLU, COUNT IT ALL JOY! Move ahead 3 spaces

HEARERS **OR** **DOERS**	**HEARERS** **OR** **DOERS**
HEARERS **OR** **DOERS**	**HEARERS** **OR** **DOERS**
HEARERS **OR** **DOERS**	**HEARERS** **OR** **DOERS**
HEARERS **OR** **DOERS**	**HEARERS** **OR** **DOERS**
HEARERS **OR** **DOERS**	**HEARERS** **OR** **DOERS**
HEARERS **OR** **DOERS**	**HEARERS** **OR** **DOERS**
HEARERS **OR** **DOERS**	**HEARERS** **OR** **DOERS**
HEARERS **OR** **DOERS**	**HEARERS** **OR** **DOERS**

ANSWERS TO PUZZLES

Answer to page 22:
Knowing that the testing of your faith produces endurance.

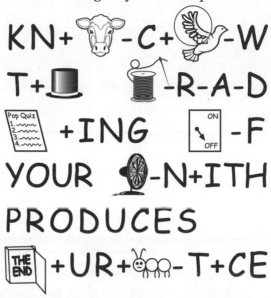

Answer to page 33:

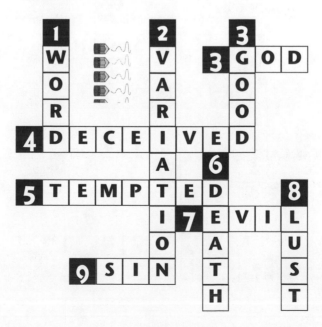

Answer to page 60:

```
B U T   T H E  W I S D O M  F R O M
2 21 20   20 8 5   23 9 19 4 15 13   6 18 15 13

A B O V E  I S  F I R S T  P U R E,
1 2 15 22 5  9 19  6 9 18 19 20  16 21 18 5

T H E N  P E A C E A B L E,
20 8  5 14  16 5 1 3 5 1  2 12 5

G E N T L E,  R E A S O N A B L E,
7  5 14 20 12 5   18 5 1 19 15 14 1 2 12 5

F U L L  O F  M E R C Y  A N D  G O O D
6 21 12 12  15 6  13 5 18 3 25  1 14 4   7 15 15 4

F R U I T S,  U N W A V E R I N G,
6 18 21 9 20 19   21 14 23 1 22 5 18 9 14 7

W I T H O U T   H Y P O C R I S Y.
23 9  20 8  15 21 20    8 25 16  15  3 18 9 19 25
```

Answer to page 63:

Answer to page 74:

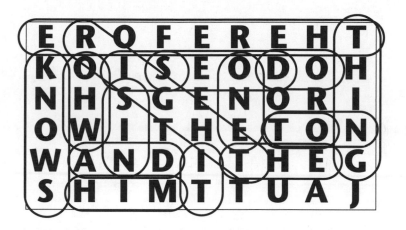

Answer to page 88:

James 5:9

```
D O   N O T   C O M P L A I N ,
4 15  14 15 20  3 15 13 16 12 1 9 14
```

```
B R E T H R E N ,   A G A I N S T   O N E
2 18 5 20 8 18 5 14   1 7 1 9 14 19 20  15 14 5
```

```
A N O T H E R ,   S O   T H A T   Y O U
1 14 15 20 8 5 18   19 15  20 8 1 20   25 15 21
```

```
Y O U R S E L V E S   M A Y   N O T   B E
25 15 21 18 19 5 12 22 5 19  13 1 25  14 15 20  2 5
```

```
J U D G E D ;   B E H O L D ,   T H E
10 21 4 7 5 4   2 5 8 15 12 4   20 8 5
```

```
J U D G E   I S   S T A N D I N G
10 21 4 7 5   9 19  19 20 1 14 4 9 14 7
```

```
R I G H T   A T   T H E   D O O R .
18 9 7 8 20   1 20   20 8 5   4 15 15 18
```

Answer to page 95:

LAST DAYS

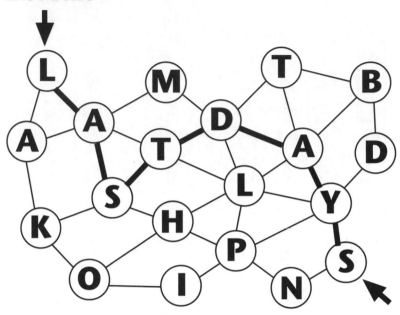

Answer to page 107:

Observation Worksheets
James

Chapter 1

1 James, a bond-servant of God and of the Lord Jesus Christ,
To the twelve tribes who are dispersed abroad: Greetings.

2 Consider it all joy, my brethren, when you encounter various trials,

3 knowing that the testing of your faith produces endurance.

4 And let endurance have its perfect result, so that you may be perfect and complete, lacking in nothing.

5 But if any of you lacks wisdom, let him ask of God, who gives to all generously and without reproach, and it will be given to him.

6 But he must *ask in faith* without any doubting, for the one who doubts is like the surf of the sea, driven and tossed by the wind.

7 For that man ought not to expect that he will receive anything from the Lord,

8 being a double-minded man, unstable in all his ways.

9 But the brother of humble circumstances is to glory in his high position;

10 and the rich man is to glory in his humiliation, because like flowering grass he will pass away.

11 For the sun rises with a scorching wind and withers the grass; and its flower falls off and the beauty of its appearance is destroyed; so too the rich man in the midst of his pursuits will fade away.

12 Blessed is a man who perseveres under trial; for once he has been approved, he will receive the crown of life which the Lord has promised to those who love Him.

13 Let no one say when he is tempted, "I am being tempted by God"; for God cannot be tempted by evil, and He Himself does not tempt anyone.

14 But each one is tempted when he is carried away and enticed by his own lust.

15 Then when lust has conceived, it gives birth to sin; and when sin is accomplished, it brings forth death.

16 Do not be deceived, my beloved brethren.

17 Every good thing given and every perfect gift is from above, coming down from the Father of lights, with whom there is no variation or shifting shadow.

18 In the exercise of His will He brought us forth by the word of truth, so that we would be a kind of first fruits among His creatures.

19 This you know, my beloved brethren. But everyone must be quick to hear, slow to speak and slow to anger;

20 for the anger of man does not achieve the righteousness of God.

21 Therefore, putting aside all filthiness and all that remains of wickedness, in humility receive the word implanted, which is able to save your souls.

22 But prove yourselves doers of the word, and not merely hearers who delude themselves.

23 For if anyone is a hearer of the word and not a doer, he is like a man who looks at his natural face in a mirror;

24 for once he has looked at himself and gone away, he has immediately forgotten what kind of person he was.

25 But one who looks intently at the perfect law, the law of liberty, and abides by it, not having become a forgetful hearer but an effectual doer, this man will be blessed in what he does.

26 If anyone thinks himself to be religious, and yet does not bridle his tongue but deceives his own heart, this man's religion is worthless.

27 Pure and undefiled religion in the sight of our God and Father is this: to visit orphans and widows in their distress, and to keep oneself unstained by the world.

Chapter 2

1 My brethren, do not hold your faith in our glorious Lord Jesus Christ with an attitude of personal favoritism.

2 For if a man comes into your assembly with a gold ring and dressed in fine clothes, and there also comes in a poor man in dirty clothes,

3 and you pay special attention to the one who is wearing the fine clothes, and say, "You sit here in a good place," and you say to the poor man, "You stand over there, or sit down by my footstool,"

4 have you not made distinctions among yourselves, and become judges with evil motives?

5 Listen, my beloved brethren: did not God choose the poor of this world to be rich in faith and heirs of the kingdom which He promised to those who love Him?

6 But you have dishonored the poor man. Is it not the rich who oppress you and personally drag you into court?

7 Do they not blaspheme the fair name by which you have been called?

8 If, however, you are fulfilling the royal law according to the Scripture, "YOU SHALL LOVE YOUR NEIGHBOR AS YOURSELF," you are doing well.

9 But if you show partiality, you are committing sin and are convicted by the law as transgressors.

10 For whoever keeps the whole law and yet stumbles in one point, he has become guilty of all.

11 For He who said, "DO NOT COMMIT ADULTERY," also said, "DO NOT

COMMIT MURDER." Now if you do not commit adultery, but do commit murder, you have become a transgressor of the law.

12 So speak and so act as those who are to be judged by the law of liberty.

13 For judgment will be merciless to one who has shown no mercy; mercy triumphs over judgment.

14 What use is it, my brethren, if someone says he has faith but he has no works? Can that faith save him?

15 If a brother or sister is without clothing and in need of daily food,

16 and one of you says to them, "Go in peace, be warmed and be filled," and yet you do not give them what is necessary for their body, what use is that?

17 Even so faith, if it has no works, is dead, being by itself.

18 But someone may well say, "You have faith and I have works; show me your faith without the works, and I will show you my faith by my works."

19 You believe that God is one. You do well; the demons also believe, and shudder.

20 But are you willing to recognize, you foolish fellow, that faith without works is useless?

21 Was not Abraham our father justified by works when he offered up Isaac his son on the altar?

22 You see that faith was working with his works, and as a result of the works, faith was perfected;

23 and the Scripture was fulfilled which says, "AND ABRAHAM BELIEVED GOD, AND IT WAS RECKONED TO HIM AS RIGHTEOUSNESS," and he was called the friend of God.

24 You see that a man is justified by works and not by faith alone.

25 In the same way, was not Rahab the harlot also justified by works when she received the messengers and sent them out by another way?

26 For just as the body without the spirit is dead, so also faith without works is dead.

Chapter 3

1 Let not many of you become teachers, my brethren, knowing that as such we will incur a stricter judgment.

2 For we all stumble in many ways. If anyone does not stumble in what he says, he is a perfect man, able to bridle the whole body as well.

3 Now if we put the bits into the horses' mouths so that they will obey us, we direct their entire body as well.

4 Look at the ships also, though they are so great and are driven by strong winds, are still directed by a very small rudder wherever the inclination of the pilot desires.

5 So also the tongue is a small part of the body, and yet it boasts of great things.

See how great a forest is set aflame by such a small fire!

6 And the tongue is a fire, the very world of iniquity; the tongue is set among our members as that which defiles the entire body, and sets on fire the course of our life, and is set on fire by hell.

7 For every species of beasts and birds, of reptiles and creatures of the sea, is tamed and has been tamed by the human race.

8 But no one can tame the tongue; it is a restless evil and full of deadly poison.

9 With it we bless our Lord and Father, and with it we curse men, who have been made in the likeness of God;

10 from the same mouth come both blessing and cursing. My brethren, these things ought not to be this way.

11 Does a fountain send out from the same opening both fresh and bitter water?

12 Can a fig tree, my brethren, produce olives, or a vine produce figs? Nor can salt water produce fresh.

13 Who among you is wise and understanding? Let him show by his good behavior his deeds in the gentleness of wisdom.

14 But if you have bitter jealousy and selfish ambition in your heart, do not be arrogant and so lie against the truth.

15 This wisdom is not that which comes down from above, but is earthly, natural, demonic.

16 For where jealousy and selfish ambition exist, there is disorder and every evil thing.

17 But the wisdom from above is first pure, then peaceable, gentle, reasonable, full of mercy and good fruits, unwavering, without hypocrisy.

18 And the seed whose fruit is righteousness is sown in peace by those who make peace.

Chapter 4

1 What is the source of quarrels and conflicts among you? Is not the source your pleasures that wage war in your members?

2 You lust and do not have; so you commit murder. You are envious and cannot obtain; so you fight and quarrel. You do not have because you do not ask.

3 You ask and do not receive, because you ask with wrong motives, so that you may spend it on your pleasures.

4 You adulteresses, do you not know that friendship with the world is hostility toward God? Therefore whoever wishes to be a friend of the world makes himself an enemy of God.

5 Or do you think that the Scripture speaks to no purpose: "He jealously desires the Spirit which He has made to dwell in us"?

6 But He gives a greater grace. Therefore it says, "GOD IS OPPOSED TO THE PROUD, BUT GIVES GRACE TO THE HUMBLE."

7 Submit therefore to God. Resist the devil and he will flee from you.

8 Draw near to God and He will draw near to you. Cleanse your hands, you sinners; and purify your hearts, you double-minded.

9 Be miserable and mourn and weep; let your laughter be turned into mourning and your joy to gloom.

10 Humble yourselves in the presence of the Lord, and He will exalt you.

11 Do not speak against one another, brethren. He who speaks against a brother or judges his brother, speaks against the law and judges the law; but if you judge the law, you are not a doer of the law but a judge of it.

12 There is only one Lawgiver and Judge, the One who is able to save and to destroy; but who are you who judge your neighbor?

13 Come now, you who say, "Today or tomorrow we will go to such and such a city, and spend a year there and engage in business and make a profit."

14 Yet you do not know what your life will be like tomorrow. You are just a vapor that appears for a little while and then vanishes away.

15 Instead, you ought to say, "If the Lord wills, we will live and also do this or that."

16 But as it is, you boast in your arrogance; all such boasting is evil.

17 Therefore, to one who knows the right thing to do and does not do it, to him it is sin.

Chapter 5

1 Come now, you rich, weep and howl for your miseries which are coming upon you.

2 Your riches have rotted and your garments have become moth-eaten.

3 Your gold and your silver have rusted; and their rust will be a witness against you and will consume your flesh like fire. It is in the last days that you have stored up your treasure!

4 Behold, the pay of the laborers who mowed your fields, and which has been withheld by you, cries out against you; and the outcry of those who did the harvesting has reached the ears of the Lord of Sabaoth.

5 You have lived luxuriously on the earth and led a life of wanton pleasure; you have fattened your hearts in a day of slaughter.

6 You have condemned and put to death the righteous man; he does not resist you.

7 Therefore be patient, brethren, until the coming of the Lord. The farmer waits for the precious produce of the soil, being patient about it, until it gets the early and late rains.

8 You too be patient; strengthen your hearts, for the coming of the Lord is near.

9 Do not complain, brethren, against one another, so that you yourselves may not be judged; behold, the Judge is standing right at the door.

10 As an example, brethren, of suffering and patience, take the prophets who spoke in the name of the Lord.

11 We count those blessed who endured. You have heard of the endurance of Job and have seen the outcome of the Lord's dealings, that the Lord is full of compassion and is merciful.

12 But above all, my brethren, do not swear, either by heaven or by earth or with any other oath; but your yes is to be yes, and your no, no, so that you may not fall under judgment.

13 Is anyone among you suffering? Then he must pray. Is anyone cheerful? He is to sing praises.

14 Is anyone among you sick? Then he must call for the elders of the church and they are to pray over him, anointing him with oil in the name of the Lord;

15 and the prayer offered in faith will restore the one who is sick, and the Lord will raise him up, and if he has committed sins, they will be forgiven him.

16 Therefore, confess your sins to one another, and pray for one another so that you may be healed. The effective prayer of a righteous man can accomplish much.

17 Elijah was a man with a nature like ours, and he prayed earnestly that it would not rain, and it did not rain on the earth for three years and six months.

18 Then he prayed again, and the sky poured rain and the earth produced its fruit.

19 My brethren, if any among you strays from the truth and one turns him back,

20 let him know that he who turns a sinner from the error of his way will save his soul from death and will cover a multitude of sins.

JOSHUA 6:17-19

Chapter 6

17 "The city shall be under the ban, it and all that is in it belongs to the LORD; only Rahab the harlot and all who are with her in the house shall live, because she hid the messengers whom we sent.

18 "But as for you, only keep yourselves from the things under the ban, so that you do not covet them and take some of the things under the ban, and make the camp of Israel accursed and bring trouble on it.

19 "But all the silver and gold and articles of bronze and iron are holy to the LORD; they shall go into the treasury of the LORD."

JOSHUA 7:1-26

Chapter 7

1 But the sons of Israel acted unfaithfully in regard to the things under the ban, for Achan, the son of Carmi, the son of Zabdi, the son of Zerah, from the tribe of Judah, took some of the things under the ban, therefore the anger of the LORD burned against the sons of Israel.

2 Now Joshua sent men from Jericho to Ai, which is near Beth-aven, east of Bethel, and said to them, "Go up and spy out the land." So the men went up and spied out Ai.

3 They returned to Joshua and said to him, "Do not let all the people go up; only about two or three thousand men need go up to Ai; do not make all the people toil up there, for they are few."

4 So about three thousand men from the people went up there, but they fled from the men of Ai.

5 The men of Ai struck down about thirty-six of their men, and pursued them from the gate as far as Shebarim and struck them

down on the descent, so the hearts of the people melted and became as water.

6 Then Joshua tore his clothes and fell to the earth on his face before the ark of the LORD until the evening, both he and the elders of Israel; and they put dust on their heads.

7 Joshua said, "Alas, O Lord GOD, why did You ever bring this people over the Jordan, only to deliver us into the hand of the Amorites, to destroy us? If only we had been willing to dwell beyond the Jordan!

8 "O Lord, what can I say since Israel has turned their back before their enemies?

9 "For the Canaanites and all the inhabitants of the land will hear of it, and they will surround us and cut off our name from the earth. And what will You do for Your great name?"

10 So the LORD said to Joshua, "Rise up! Why is it that you have fallen on your face?

11 "Israel has sinned, and they have also transgressed My covenant which I commanded them. And they have even taken some of the things under the ban and have both stolen and deceived. Moreover, they have also put them among their own things.

12 "Therefore the sons of Israel cannot stand before their enemies; they turn their backs before their enemies, for they have become accursed. I will not be with you anymore unless you destroy the things under the ban from your midst.

13 "Rise up! Consecrate the people and say, "Consecrate yourselves for tomorrow, for thus the LORD, the God of Israel, has said, "There are things under the ban in your midst, O Israel. You cannot stand before your enemies until you have removed the things under the ban from your midst."

14 'In the morning then you shall come near by your tribes. And it shall be that the tribe which the LORD takes by lot shall come near by families, and the family which the LORD takes shall come near by households, and the household which the LORD takes shall come near man by man.

15 'It shall be that the one who is taken with the things under the ban shall be burned with fire, he and all that belongs to him, because he has transgressed the covenant of the LORD, and because he has committed a disgraceful thing in Israel.'"

16 So Joshua arose early in the morning and brought Israel near by tribes, and the tribe of Judah was taken.

17 He brought the family of Judah near, and he took the family of the Zerahites; and he brought the family of the Zerahites near man by man, and Zabdi was taken.

18 He brought his household near man by man; and Achan, son of Carmi, son of Zabdi, son of Zerah, from the tribe of Judah, was taken.

19 Then Joshua said to Achan, "My son, I implore you, give glory to the LORD, the God of Israel, and give praise to Him; and tell me now what you have done. Do not hide it from me."

20 So Achan answered Joshua and said, "Truly, I have sinned against the LORD, the God of Israel, and this is what I did:

21 when I saw among the spoil a beautiful mantle from Shinar and two hundred shekels of silver and a bar of gold fifty shekels in weight, then I coveted them and took them; and behold, they are concealed in the earth inside my tent with the silver underneath it."

22 So Joshua sent messengers, and they ran to the tent; and behold, it was concealed in his tent with the silver underneath it.

23 They took them from inside the tent and brought them to Joshua

and to all the sons of Israel, and they poured them out before the LORD.

24 Then Joshua and all Israel with him, took Achan the son of Zerah, the silver, the mantle, the bar of gold, his sons, his daughters, his oxen, his donkeys, his sheep, his tent and all that belonged to him; and they brought them up to the valley of Achor.

25 Joshua said, "Why have you troubled us? The LORD will trouble you this day." And all Israel stoned them with stones; and they burned them with fire after they had stoned them with stones.

26 They raised over him a great heap of stones that stands to this day, and the LORD turned from the fierceness of His anger. Therefore the name of that place has been called the valley of Achor to this day.

INDUCTIVE BIBLE STUDIES
DISCOVER 4 YOURSELF®
FOR KIDS!

BRING THE WHOLE COUNSEL OF GOD'S WORD TO KIDS!

▼ GENESiS
God's Amazing Creation (Genesis 1–2)
Digging Up the Past (Genesis 3–11)
Abraham, God's Brave Explorer (Genesis 11–25)
Extreme Adventures with God (Genesis 24–36)
Joseph, God's Superhero (Genesis 37–50)

 ◄ 2 TiMOTHY
Becoming God's Champion

 ◄ jAMES
Boy, Have I Got Problems!

ESTHER ►
God Has Big Plans for You, Esther

 ◄ REVELATiON
Bible Prophecy for Kids
(Revelation 1–7)
A Sneak Peek into the Future
(Revelation 8–22)

DANiEL ►
You're a Brave Man, Daniel!
(Daniel 1–6)
Fast-Forward to the Future
(Daniel 7–12)

▲ TOPiCAL & SKiLLS
God, What's Your Name? (Names of God)
Lord, Teach Me to Pray (for Kids)
How to Study Your Bible (for Kids)
  also available in DVD
Cracking the Covenant Code (for Kids)

jONAH ►
Wrong Way, Jonah!

◄ GOSPEL OF jOHN
Jesus in the Spotlight (John 1–10)
Jesus—Awesome Power, Awesome Love (John 11–16)
Jesus—To Eternity and Beyond (John 17–21)